MICHIGAN BUSINESS
REPORTS   Number 59

Mergers in the Savings and Loan Industry

Structural Changes, Financial Comparisons, and the
Performance of Merging Savings and Loan Associations

WILLIAM D. BRADFORD

A publication of the
Division of Research
Graduate School of Business Administration
The University of Michigan
Ann Arbor, Michigan

ABSTRACT

First, this study analyzes the financial and charter-ownership characteristics of the acquiring and acquired savings and loan associations (S&Ls) involved in nonsupervisory mergers from January 1969 through December 1974. Specifically, the differences between the acquiring and acquired S&Ls in regard to their characteristics are analyzed. Then the asset sizes of the S&Ls involved in mergers are examined. Thereafter, financial characteristics are examined to identify the differences between the acquiring and acquired associations.

Secondly, this study compares the financial characteristics and performance of a large group of acquiring S&Ls to a matching group of nonmerging S&Ls. The comparisons relate to the year preceding the merger of the acquiring S&L, and to a two-year and a three-year period following the year of the merger.

Mergers in the industry are shown to have tended to shift industry assets toward direct regulation by the Federal Home Loan Bank Board and away from state regulation. Also acquiring associations are found to be more efficient in an operating sense and to have mortgage distributions and financing patterns which are significantly different from those of acquired associations.

With respect to the comparisons between acquiring S&Ls and comparable nonmerging S&Ls the acquiring S&Ls are found to differ significantly from the nonmerging S&Ls in several areas of both asset distribution and operational performance. This comparision held true both for the year preceding the mergers, and for the two- and three-year periods following the mergers.

Some conclusions about the policy implications of these results are discussed.

ACKNOWLEDGEMENTS

Much of the research on which this monograph reports was conducted while I served as Visiting Economist, Office of Economic Research, Federal Home Loan Bank Board, under a Sears Roebuck Foundation—AACSB Faculty Fellowship. Programming assistance was provided at the Bank Board by Rita Ferrara, to whom I am greatly indebted. I am also indebted to Harris Friedman and Donald Kaplan of the Bank Board's Office of Economic Research for their support. Research support at Stanford was provided by the Dean Witter Foundation and the General Electric Company, and programming assistance at Stanford was provided by Eduardo Costa. The views expressed are solely my own, and do not necessarily reflect those of the organizations mentioned.

CONTENTS

TABLES

I

INTRODUCTION

Background

In recent years, mergers of savings and loan associations (S&Ls) have been an important medium of change in the savings and loan industry. From January 1, 1969, to December 31, 1974, there were 540 mergers in the United States involving FSLIC-insured savings and loan associations.[1] Table 1 breaks down these mergers by year and Federal Home Loan Bank district. This rate of mergers is significant in several respects. First, the average annual merger rate during this period is over three times that of insured associations during 1960-68.[2] Second, Federal Home Loan Bank Board (FHLBB) officials anticipate that the merger rate of 1969-74 will be maintained over the next five to ten years. Thus, this level of mergers and its effect on the industry is at least a semipermanent phenomenon. Third, if the savings and loan industry continues to increase its share of the resources of all financial institutions while decreasing in absolute number, then it will undoubtedly become necessary to consider the anti-competitive effects of merger in the industry.

Thus, it should be anticipated that a growing concern about mergers in the savings and loan industry will occur over the next decade. However, despite the importance of mergers in the recent past and their importance in the near future, only a limited amount of quantitative data has been presented concerning the characteristics of merging savings and loan associations.

In this regard, a knowledge of the characteristics of merging savings and loan associations is an important prerequisite to an understanding of mergers per se and, more importantly, to an understanding of the impact of mergers on the structure of the savings and loan industry. Additionally, such knowledge would contribute to a more informed merger policy for regulators of the industry.

1

Therefore, this study analyzes the financial relationships and charter-ownership characteristics of 510 of the 540 mergers of FSLIC-insured savings and loans which occured from January 1, 1969, through December 31, 1974. The thirty associations not included consist of twenty-eight which are regarded as supervisory mergers, and two for which data are not available.[4] Table 2 gives the type and year of the regular mergers in 1969-74.

Organization of the study

In this study, Chapter 2 will discuss structural changes related to the merger movement in the industry. First, the type of charter (federal or state) and of ownership (stock or mutual) of the acquired and acquiring S&Ls will be compared. This analysis will specify the charter-ownership trends which have developed through merger movement and will identify areas of greater concentration because of merger. It also will examine the acquired and acquiring S&Ls for asset size differences and for how these differences are distributed among charter types and ownership types.

Chapter 3 compares the financial characteristics of the acquiring and acquired S&Ls. A *t*-test is used to determine whether the observed differences between the means of ratios are the result of sampling variation. Although we have eliminated those mergers resulting from financial problems (at least as interpreted by the FHLBB), differences may exist between the acquiring and acquired association because of the clientele each serves and the way in which each is managed.

Chapter 4 compares the financial characteristics and performance of acquiring S&Ls to a matched group of nonmerging S&Ls during the year preceding the year of merger and two and three years after the year of merger. Since the acquiring S&Ls and matching nonmerging associations should be relatively similar because of the criteria by which the latter were chosen, the relative performance of the two groups of S&Ls can provide insight into unique characteristics of acquiring S&Ls and the effect of merger on the performance of merging savings and loan associations. Chapter 5 contains the conclusions of the study.

Table 1

MERGERS OF INSURED SAVINGS AND LOAN ASSOCIATIONS,
1969 THROUGH 1974

Year	Boston	New York	Pitts-burgh	Atlanta	Cin-cinnati	Indian-apolis	Chicago	Des Moines	Little Rock	Topeka	San Francisco	Seattle	Row Total	Supervisory Mergers
1969	4	5	7	7	5	2	1	0	1	0	18	2	52	5
1970	4	9	13	8	6	4	12	4	2	3	20	2	87	9
1971	0	17	21	9	16	6	11	3	1	5	22	7	118	2
1972	2	10	9	13	3	2	13	3	2	4	21	4	86	3
1973	0	13	10	8	5	2	17	5	1	3	9	2	75	6
1974	1	13	15	28	12	2	20	10	2	5	10	4	122	3
Totals	11	67	75	73	47	18	74	25	9	20	100	21	540	28

Source: Federal Home Loan Bank Board

Table 2

REGULAR MERGERS OF INSURED SAVINGS AND LOAN ASSOCIATIONS, 1969 THROUGH 1974

Year	Federal*	State Charter			Total per Year	Average Number of Associations	Merger Rate (in percentage)
		Mutual	Stock	All			
1969	14 (11)	14 (16)	19 (20)	33 (36)	47	4454	1.0
1970	38 (26)	24 (32)	16 (20)	40 (52)	78	4402	1.8
1971	64 (23)	32 (61)	20 (32)	52 (93)	116	4318	2.7
1972	28 (18)	28 (35)	27 (30)	55 (65)	83	4231	2.0
1973	40 (20)	20 (39)	9 (10)	29 (49)	69	4177	1.7
1974	67 (50)	38 (47)	13 (21)	51 (68)	118	4152	2.8
Total	250 (147)	156 (230)	104 (133)	260 (363)	510	4291	12.0
Average Number of Associations	2056	1611	524	2255	...	...	...
Total Merger Rate 1969-1974	12.2 (7.1)	9.7 (14.3)	16.7 (21.3)	11.6 (16.2)	...	...	...

Source: Federal Home Loan Bank Board
*Numbers in parentheses represent data on *acquired* associations.

NOTES

1. For the purpose of this study, a merger is defined as any form of combination wherein two or more associations are joined together under the same charter.

2. The annual merger rate is defined as the number of mergers during the year divided by the average number of associations during the year (the number at the start of the year plus the number at year-end divided by 2).

3. See Federal Reserve Bank of Cleveland, "Bank Merger Activity in the Fourth Federal Reserve District, 1960-1967," *Economic Review*, Mar. 1969; P.M. Horvitz and B. Schull, "The Impact of Branch Banking on Bank Performance," *National Banking Review*, Dec. 1964; D. L. Smith, *Characteristics of Merging Banks* (Washington, D.C. Board of Governors of the Federal Reserve System, 1969); and S.A. Rhodes and A.J. Yeats, "Growth, Consolidation, and Mergers in Banking." *Journal of Finance*, Dec. 1974, for corresponding analyses in the commercial banking industry.

4. A supervisory merger refers to one in which the disappearing association is judged by the Federal Home Loan Bank Board to be in serious financial condition because of violation of operating procedures, operating conditions, or failure to meet insurability requirements. The financial condition may threaten continuation of operations, and thus is considered to endanger depositors (and FSLIC). The normal consequence is that the supervisory agents urge a merger as the best (or only) solution. See E.F. Brigham and R.R. Pettit, "Effects of Structure on Performance of the Savings and Loan Industry," in *Study of the Savings and Loan Industry*, ed. by Irwin Friend (Washington, D.C.: Government Printing Office, 1969), p. 1054.

II

TYPE AND SIZE OF ACQUIRING AND ACQUIRED ASSOCIATIONS

Only two previous studies have attempted to analyze the effect of mergers on the savings and loan industry. Gillies and Mittelbach conducted a descriptive study about the merger movement of the savings and loan industry in California through 1957.[1] Brigham and Pettit conducted several analyses of mergers in the savings and loan industry for the entire United States, dealing mainly with the 1958 to 1967 period[2]. This section will analyze several of the hypotheses presented in their study.

Specifically, Brigham and Pettit concluded that:

  1. The form of ownership, mutual or stock, affects the rate of merger activity, with stock S&Ls being more actively engaged in mergers.
  2. The type of charter, federal or state, is not a significant determinant of merger activity among mutual savings and loan associations.[3]

Let us first analyze these conclusions on the basis of the results of the mergers in the S&L industry from 1969 through 1974. Then we will analyze asset-size difference between acquiring and acquired S&Ls for the different types of savings and loans.

The Effect of Ownership on Merger Rates

Background

The hypothesis concerning form of ownership and merger rates, which Brigham and Pettit found to hold in 1958-67, was invalid for 1969-74. Brigham and Pettit suggested the following as reasons for the higher merger rate of stock S&Ls:

...First, failing firms are more likely to seek mergers or to be amenable to merger proposals, and FHLBB policy is much more lenient toward failing-firm than healthy-firm mergers. Stock S&Ls are mostly located in areas of the country where economic conditions have been less stable, and stock companies are also more aggressive and take more risks than

7

mutuals. Both of these factors cause a higher rate of merger activity among stock than mutual firms. Financial problems are not the entire answer to the higher merger rate among stock firms; however, healthy stock companies have a higher merger rate than healthy mutuals, both nationwide and in given market areas. Our analysis suggests that compensating those in control of an acquired association is frequently easier to work out in the case of a stock company than it is in the case of a mutual.[4]

Brigham and Pettit's argument on the similarity of merger rates for federally chartered S&Ls and state chartered mutual S&Ls is as follows:

> ...The FHLBB has total authority over mergers involving Federal S&Ls and, through the FSLIC, ultimate authority over insured State associations. Because of this dominant role over virtually all associations, one could hypothesize that the rate of merger activity would be similar for both state and federally chartered mutual S&Ls, as similar incentives to merge and a uniform FHLBB merger policy could be expected to produce a similar rate in both mutual segments of the industry.[5]

Two events subsequent to the period of the Brigham and Pettit study, have affected the applicability of their conclusions to the industry today.

First, the McFadden Act of 1927, which requires that commercial bank regulatory agencies defer to state branching laws, is not applicable to Federal Home Loan Bank Board decisions concerning branching of federally chartered S&Ls, all of which were mutual until 1974. Starting in the late 1960s the Board used this situation to allow federally chartered S&Ls to branch by merging or establishing new facilities in some states where branching of state-chartered S&Ls is not allowed. The Board has justified its actions as increasing the ability of S&Ls to compete with other types of institutions for savings funds and investment opportunities.[6] Secondly, the denial rate of merger applications has been decreasing since the late 1960s. Table 3 shows this rate for 1969 through 1974. In no year does the denial rate exceed 8 percent, and the rate appears to show a downward trend over the period. Federal associations are the major beneficiaries of a liberalization of merger policy since the Board is the only agency to which federal S&Ls must apply for merger approvals. State S&Ls, in comparison, must apply to both the Board and the relevant state regulatory agency for merger approval.

Another significant factor in examining merger rates of the different S&Ls is the basis on which mergers are analyzed. Merger rates can be specified in terms of the type of S&L being acquired or the type of S&L which is acquiring. Each will present a different result. The first exhibit in Table 4, which is an aggregate cross tabulation of mergers for 1969 through 1974 by type, shows that the type breakdown of acquiring and acquired S&Ls is unevenly distributed. Tables 5 through 10 give this information on a yearly basis. For example, 49 percent of all acquiring (surviving) S&Ls were federal whereas only 29 percent of the acquired

Table 3
FEDERAL HOME LOAN BANK SYSTEM
APPROVALS AND DENIALS OF MERGER
APPLICATIONS, 1969 THROUGH 1974

Year	Applications	Denials	Denial Rate (in percentage)
1969	83	6	7.23
1970	132	8	6.06
1971	118	6	5.08
1972	103	4	3.88
1973	124	4	3.23
1974	132	4	3.03

Source: Federal Home Loan Bank Board

(disappearing) S&Ls were federal in 1969-1974. Given this situation, our analysis will determine merger rates of different types of associations as both acquiring and acquired S&Ls.

Findings

The annual number of mergers and the merger rate for each type of S&L (both as acquiring and as acquired partner) is shown in Table 11. Mann-Whitney U tests were conducted to determine whether the annual merger rates were significantly different over the period.[7] Table 12 shows the results. Brigham and Pettit based their analysis on a definition of merger rates in terms of the rate at which a particular type of association *acquires* S&Ls. Given this definition, we can reject the null hypothesis of the equality of merger rates of the different S&L types only when we compare state stock and state mutual associations. State stock S&Ls have a greater merger rate than state mutual S&Ls at a 0.05 significance level. The result that the merger rate of stock associations is not significantly higher than that of federal associatons or all mutual associations contradicts the conclusions arrived at by Brigham and Pettit.

If we consider a merger rate as based on the rate at which a particular type of association is *acquired*, results opposite to those of Brigham and Pettit are also found. First, the merger rates of state mutual S&Ls and state stock S&Ls are not found to be significantly different. Second, the

Table 4

GENERAL COMPARISONS OF MERGERS IN THE SAVINGS & LOAN INDUSTRY,
DECEMBER 1969 - DECEMBER 1974

Acquired Association	Distribution by Type Acquiring Association			Row Total	Percentage of All S&L Mergers
	Federal	State Stock	State Mutual		
Federal	125	0	22	147	28.8
State Stock	25	104	4	133	26.1
State Mutual	100	0	130	230	45.1
Total	250	104	156	510	
Percentage	49.0	20.4	30.6		100.0

Distribution by Assets Size
(Total Assets in $ Millions)

Acquired Association	Acquiring Association								Row Total	Percentage of All S&L Mergers
	0 to 5.0	5.1 to 10.0	10.1 to 15.0	15.1 to 25.0	25.1 to 50.0	50.1 to 100.0	100.1 to 200.0	Over 200.0		
0-5.0	8	18	16	15	30	38	14	14	153	30.0
5.1-10.0	1	5	3	17	22	22	12	24	106	20.8
10.1-15.0	...	...	2	4	6	10	7	16	45	8.8

								Total	Percentage
15.1-25.0	...	1	7	8	17	9	25	68	13.3
25.1-50.0	2	...	...	8	9	14	44	77	15.1
50.1-100.0	...	...	1	1	3	5	29	39	7.6
100.1-200.0	...	1	1	...	1	4	7	14	2.7
Over 200.0	...	...	...	2	...	1	5	8	1.6
Total	11	25	45	77	100	66	164	510	
Percentage	2.2	4.9	8.8	15.1	19.6	12.9	32.2		100.0

Median Asset Sizes
(in Millions of Dollars)*

Type of Acquired Association	Type of Acquiring Association		
	Federal	State Stock	State Mutual
Federal	159.5	A†	37.3
	14.7		15.4
State stock	413.3	203.8	A
	11.6	27.9	
State mutual	69.6	A	33.2
	4.7		5.3

Overall Median: Acquiring Association 84.2
Acquired Association 9.8

*Acquiring association above, acquired association below.
†A = fewer than five S&Ls.

Table 5
ANALYSIS OF SAVINGS & LOAN MERGERS IN 1969

Distribution by Type

Acquired Association	Acquiring Association			Row Total	Percentage of All S&L Mergers
	Federal	State Stock	State Mutual		
Federal	7	0	4	11	23.4
State Stock	1	19	0	20	42.6
State Mutual	6	0	10	16	34.0
Total	14	19	14	47	
Percentage	29.8	40.4	29.8		100.0

Distribution by Assets Size
(Total Assets in $ Millions)

Acquired Association	Acquiring Association								Row Total	Percentage of All S&L Mergers
	0 to 5.0	5.1 to 10.0	10.1 to 15.0	15.1 to 25.0	25.1 to 50.0	50.1 to 100.0	100.1 to 200.0	Over 200.0		
0-5.0	...	4	1	2	2	5	...	...	14	29.8
5.1-10.0	1	...	...	3	1	2	1	1	9	19.1
10.1-15.0	...	...	...	1	1	2	...	...	4	8.5

									Total	Percentage
15.1–25.0	…	…	…	1	…	4	…	2	7	14.9
25.1–50.0	…	…	…	…	…	1	3	1	5	10.6
50.1–100.0	…	…	…	…	…	1	…	3	4	8.5
100.1–200.0	…	…	…	…	…	1	1	1	3	6.4
Over 200.0	…	…	…	…	…	…	…	1	1	2.1
Total	1	4	1	7	5	15	5	9	47	
Percentage	2.1	8.5	2.1	14.9	10.6	31.9	10.6	19.1		100.0

Median Asset Sizes
(in Millions of Dollars*)

Type of Acquired Association	Type of Acquiring Association		
	Federal	State Stock	State Mutual
Federal	73.4 / 24.1	A†	25.8 / 10.5
State stock	A	108.3 / 24.2	A
State mutual	37.6 / 1.9	A	21.3 / 3.9

Overall Median: Acquiring Association 65.4
Acquired Association 10.3

*Acquiring S&L above, acquired S&L below.
†A = fewer than five S&Ls.

Table 6
ANALYSIS OF SAVINGS & LOAN MERGERS IN 1970

Distribution by Type

Acquired Association	Acquiring Association			Row Total	Percentage of All S&L Mergers
	Federal	State Stock	State Mutual		
Federal	21	0	5	26	33.3
State Stock	4	16	0	20	25.6
State Mutual	13	0	19	32	41.1
Total	38	16	24	78	
Percentage	48.7	20.5	30.8		100.0

Distribution by Assets Size
(Total Assets in $ Millions)

Acquired Association	Acquiring Association								Row Total	Percentage of All S&L Mergers
	0 to 5.0	5.1 to 10.0	10.1 to 15.0	15.1 to 25.0	25.1 to 50.0	50.1 to 100.0	100.1 to 200.0	Over 200.0		
0-5.0	1	4	4	...	4	3	1	2	19	24.4
5.1-10.0	...	2	1	2	2	2	4	5	18	23.1
10.1-15.0	...	...	...	3	1	2	2	3	11	14.1

									Total	%
15.1-25.0	...	...	...	2	2	1	4	4	13	16.1
25.1-50.0	...	...	...	...	2	2	4	2	10	12.8
50.1-100.0	...	...	...	...	...	...	1	3	4	5.1
100.1-200.0	...	...	...	1	...	...	3	...	3	3.8
Over 200.0	...	...	...	...	...	...	...	...	0	...
Total	1	6	5	8	11	10	18	19	78	
Percentage	1.3	7.7	6.4	10.3	14.1	12.8	23.1	24.4		100.0

Median Asset Sizes
(in Millions of Dollars*)

Type of Acquired Association	Type of Acquiring Association		
	Federal	State Stock	State Mutual
Federal	119.9 12.2	A†	23.5 17.2
State stock	354.0 10.6	156.6 27.6	A
State mutual	56.9 4.7	A	32.2 6.3

Overall Median: Acquiring Association 88.8
Acquired Association 10.3

*Acquiring S&L above, acquired S&L below.
†A = less than five S&Ls.

Table 7
ANALYSIS OF SAVINGS & LOAN MERGERS IN 1971

Distribution by Type

Acquired Association	Acquiring Association				Percentage of All S&L Mergers
	Federal	State Stock	State Mutual	Row Total	
Federal	20	0	3	23	19.8
State Stock	11	20	1	32	27.6
State Mutual	33	0	28	61	52.6
Total	64	20	32	116	
Percentage	55.2	17.2	27.6		100.0

Distribution by Assets Size
(Total Assets in $ Millions)

Acquired Association	Acquiring Association								Row Total	Percentage of All S&L Mergers
	0 to 5.0	5.1 to 10.0	10.1 to 15.0	15.1 to 25.0	25.1 to 50.0	50.1 to 100.0	100.1 to 200.0	Over 200.0		
0-5.0	3	6	5	4	12	10	4	6	50	43.1
5.1-10.0	...	...	1	2	4	3	2	5	17	14.7
10.1-15.0	...	...	...	...	1	3	...	4	8	6.9

									Total	Percentage
15.1-25.0	...	1	...	1	...	5	4	5	16	13.8
25.1-50.0	1	...	...	...	1	3	5	10	20	17.2
50.1-100.0	...	...	...	...	...	...	...	2	2	1.7
100.1-200.0	...	1	...	...	...	...	1	1	3	2.6
Over 200.0	...	...	...	...	...	...	...	0	0	...
Total	4	8	6	7	18	24	16	33	116	
Percentage	3.4	6.9	5.2	6.0	15.5	20.7	13.8	28.4	100.0	

Median Asset Sizes
(in Millions of Dollars*)

Type of Acquired Association	Type of Acquiring Association		
	Federal	State Stock	State Mutual
Federal	98.1 4.5	A†	A
State stock	22.1 10.9	23.8 22.2	A
State mutual	65.9 4.1	A	23.7 4.2

Overall Median: Acquiring Association 69.4
Acquired Association 7.0

*Acquiring S&L above, acquired S&L below.
†A = fewer than five S&Ls.

Table 8
ANALYSIS OF SAVINGS & LOAN MERGERS IN 1972

Distribution by Type

Acquired Association	Acquiring Association			Row Total	Percentage of All S&L Mergers
	Federal	State Stock	State Mutual		
Federal	16	0	2	18	21.7
State Stock	2	27	1	30	36.1
State Mutual	10	0	25	35	42.2
Total	28	27	28	83	
Percentage	33.7	32.5	33.7		100.0

*Distribution by Assets Size
(Total Assets in $ Millions)*

Acquired Association	Acquiring Association								Row Total	Percentage of All S&L Mergers
	0 to 5.0	5.1 to 10.0	10.1 to 15.0	15.1 to 25.0	25.1 to 50.0	50.1 to 100.0	100.1 to 200.0	Over 200.0		
0-5.0	3	1	1	3	1	5	4	1	19	22.9
5.1-10.0	...	1	...	3	4	4	2	3	17	20.5
10.1-15.0	...	...	...	2	...	1	2	4	9	10.8

								Total	Percentage
15.1–25.0	⋯	⋯	⋯	2	3	3	1	⋯	9	10.8
25.1–50.0	1	⋯	⋯	⋯	1	1	⋯	10	13	15.7
50.1–100.0	⋯	⋯	⋯	2	1	2	⋯	7	12	14.5
100.1–200.0	⋯	⋯	⋯	⋯	⋯	⋯	⋯	1	1	1.2
Over 200.0	⋯	⋯	⋯	2	⋯	⋯	1	⋯	3	3.6
Total	4	2	1	8	14	16	10	28	83	
Percentage	4.8	2.4	1.2	9.6	16.9	19.3	12.0	33.7		100.0

Median Asset Sizes
(in Millions of Dollars*)

Type of Acquired Association	Type of Acquiring Association		
	Federal	State Stock	State Mutual
Federal	236.7 / 26.9	A†	A
State stock	A	235.4 / 36.7	A
State mutual	64.7 / 4.1	A	48.7 / 6.0

Overall Median: Acquiring Association 84.5 / Acquired Association 13.4

*Acquiring S&L above, acquired S&L below.

†A = fewer than five S&Ls.

Table 9
ANALYSIS OF SAVINGS & LOAN MERGERS IN 1973

Distribution by Type

| | Acquiring Association | | | | |
Acquired Association	Federal	State Stock	State Mutual	Row Total	Percentage of All S&L Mergers
Federal	17	0	3	20	29.0
State Stock	1	9	0	10	14.5
State Mutual	22	0	17	39	...
Total	40	9	20	69	
Percentage	58.0	13.0	29.0		100.0

Distribution by Assets Size
(Total Assets in $ Millions)

| | Acquiring Association | | | | | | | | | |
Acquired Association	0 to 5.0	5.1 to 10.0	10.1 to 15.0	15.1 to 25.0	25.1 to 50.0	50.1 to 100.0	100.1 to 200.0	Over 200.0	Row Total	Percentage of All S&Ls Mergers
0-5.0	...	2	4	3	3	4	4	3	23	33.3
5.1-10.0	...	1	...	2	6	4	...	5	18	26.1
10.1-15.0	...	...	1	...	...	1	3	2	7	10.1

							Total	Percentage
15.1-25.0	...	...	...	1	2	1	5	9	13.0
25.1-50.0	...	...	...	...	1	...	5	6	8.7
50.1-100.0	...	...	1	...	...	...	3	4	5.8
100.1-200.0	...	...	...	...	...	...	...	0	...
Over 200.0	...	...	...	...	...	2	2	2	2.9
Total	3	5	6	10	12	8	25	69	
Percentage	4.3	7.2	8.7	14.5	17.4	11.6	36.2		100.0

*Median Asset Sizes
(in Millions of Dollars*)*

	Type of Acquiring Association		
Type of Acquired Association	Federal	State Stock	State Mutual
Federal	134.7 / 9.8	A†	A
State stock	A	385.0 / 38.9	A
State mutual	96.7 / 6.1	A	36.9 / 4.7

Overall Median: Acquiring Association 95.2
Acquired Association 8.6

*Acquiring S&L above, acquired S&L below.
†A = fewer than five S&Ls.

Table 10
ANALYSIS OF SAVINGS & LOAN MERGERS IN 1974

Distribution by Type

Acquired Association	Acquiring Association			Row Total	Percentage of All S&L Mergers
	Federal	State Stock	State Mutual		
Federal	45	0	5	50	42.4
State Stock	6	13	2	21	17.8
State Mutual	16	0	31	47	39.8
Total	67	13	38	118	
Percentage	56.8	11.0	32.2		100.0

Distribution by Assets Size
(Total Assets in $ Millions)

Acquired Association	Acquiring Association								Row Total	Percentage of All S&L Mergers
	0 to 5.0	5.1 to 10.0	10.1 to 15.0	15.1 to 25.0	25.1 to 50.1	50.1 to 100.0	100.1 to 200.0	Over 200.0		
0-5.0	1	1	1	3	8	11	1	3	29	24.5
5.1-10.0	...	1	1	5	5	7	3	5	27	22.9
10.1-15.0	...	...	1	...	1	1	...	3	6	5.1

									Total	Percentage
15.1-25.0	...	...	1	1	2	2	...	8	14	11.9
25.1-50.0	...	...	...	...	3	2	2	16	23	19.5
50.1-100.0	...	...	...	...	...	...	2	11	13	11.0
100.1-200.0	...	...	...	...	...	...	...	4	4	3.4
Over 200.0	...	...	...	...	...	...	1	1	2	1.7
Total	1	2	4	9	19	23	9	51	118	
Percentage	0.8	1.7	3.4	7.6	16.1	19.5	7.6	43.2		100.0

Median Asset Sizes
(in Millions of Dollars*)

Type of Acquired Association	Type of Acquiring Association		
	Federal	State Stock	State Mutual
Federal	296.3 22.8	A†	34.5 12.2
State stock	1,262.1 25.6	253.9 22.6	A
State mutual	127.3 8.5	A	50.7 6.4

Overall Median: Acquiring Association 126.7
Acquired Association 12.5

*Acquiring S&L above, acquired S&L below.
†A = fewer than five S&Ls.

Table 11

RATES OF REGULAR MERGERS FOR INSURED
SAVINGS AND LOAN ASSOCIATIONS, 1969 THROUGH 1974
(In Percentage)

| Year | Federal* | State Charter | | |
		Mutual	Stock	All
1969	0.67 (0.53)	0.81 (0.93)	2.84 (2.99)	1.41 (1.54)
1970	1.83 (1.25)	1.42 (1.90)	2.46 (3.08)	1.71 (2.22)
1971	3.10 (1.11)	1.95 (3.73)	3.20 (5.12)	2.37 (4.25)
1972	1.37 (0.88)	1.76 (2.20)	4.50 (5.00)	2.51 (2.97)
1973	1.96 (0.98)	1.29 (2.51)	1.52 (1.69)	1.35 (2.29)
1974	3.26 (2.43)	2.52 (3.12)	2.17 (3.50)	2.43 (3.24)

Source: Federal Home Loan Bank Board.
Note: Regular merger rates are defined as nonsupervisory and non-FSLIC —assisted
mergers during the year divided by the average number of associations during
the year.
*The numbers in parentheses represent data on *acquired* associations.

merger rate of state mutual S&Ls is found to be higher than that of
federal S&Ls at less than a 0.01 level of significance. Thus, the merger
policy of the Board during 1969-74 has resulted in a relationship of
merger rates among the associations which is different from that in the
period analyzed by Brigham and Pettit (1958-67).

We also can examine the overall structure of the savings and loan
industry as affected by mergers. Table 13 shows the number of total
insured S&Ls and the breakdown by type at year-end 1968 through 1974;
Table 14 gives the breakdown by state for year-end 1968 and year-end
1974. Although 147 federal S&Ls were acquired over the period, a merger
rate of 7.1 percent (see Table 4), the total number of federal S&Ls
declined by only 0.14 percent. State stock S&Ls declined by 10.5 percent,
from 676 to 605, although they experienced a merger rate of 21.3 percent.
However, the 14.7 percent decline in the number of state mutual S&Ls
from 1,731 to 1,476 was the largest of the three types, and they had a

Table 12

DIFFERENCES IN 1969-74 ANNUAL MERGER RATES

Calculated by Mann-Whitney U Tests,
1969-1974

Type of Association	Mann-Whitney U Statistic
Acquiring	
Federal and State Mutual	13
State Stock and Federal	11
State Stock and State Mutual	5*
All State-Chartered and Federal	17
State Stock and All Mutual	10
Acquired	
State Mutual and Federal	2**
State Stock and Federal	1**
State Stock and State Mutual	10
All State-Chartered and Federal	3**
State Stock and All Mutual	2**

Note: The U statistics were calculated under the null hypothesis that the annual merger rates of the two groups are equal. The alternate hypothesis in each case is that the acquirers' merger rate is greater than the acquireds' merger rate.
*Significant at the 0.05 level
**Significant at the 0.01 level

Table 13

INSURED SAVINGS AND LOAN ASSOCIATIONS
31 December 1968 - 31 December 1974

Type	1968	1969	1970	1971	1972	1973	1974
Total Insured	4,470	4,438	4,365	4,271	4,191	4,163	4,141
Federal	2,063	2,071	2,067	2,049	2,038	2,041	2,060
State Mutual	1,731	1,706	1,662	1,608	1,566	1,530	1,476
State Stock	676	661	636	614	587	592	605

Source: Federal Home Loan Bank Board.

Table 14
INSURED SAVINGS AND LOAN ASSOCIATIONS BY STATE, 1968 AND 1974

State	State Stock		Federal		State Mutual		Total	
	1968*	1974*	1968*	1974*	1968*	1974*	1968*	1974*
Connecticut	...	...	18	19	20	17	38	36
Maine	...	...	9	9	19	12	28	21
Massachusetts	...	...	35	34	1	1	36	35
New Hampshire	...	...	7	7	13	11	20	18
Rhode Island	...	...	2	2	6	4	8	6
Vermont	...	...	2	2	6	5	8	7
District 1 Total	...	...	73	73	65	50	138	123
New Jersey	...	...	26	23	195	166	221	189
New York	...	...	85	83	111	71	196	154
Puerto Rico	...	...	9	11	...	...	9	11
Virgin Islands	...	...	...	...	...	...	...	...
District 2 Total	...	...	120	117	306	237	426	354
Delaware	...	...	3	2	2	2	5	4
Pennsylvania	...	...	134	115	186	161	320	276
West Virginia	...	...	23	28	7	2	30	30
District 3 Total	...	...	160	145	195	165	355	310
Alabama	...	...	49	56	8	6	57	62
Dist. of Columbia	...	...	9	12	14	4	23	16
Florida	...	...	129	127	5	5	134	132
Georgia	...	...	100	97	4	2	104	99
Maryland	...	...	65	57	21	21	86	78
North Carolina	...	...	37	41	133	122	170	163
South Carolina	...	...	47	48	24	23	71	71
Virginia	18	28	32	30	15	15	65	73
District 4 Total	18	28	468	468	224	198	710	694
Kentucky	...	...	89	92	14	14	103	106
Ohio	87	77	138	135	125	106	350	318
Tennessee	...	...	70	76	...	...	70	76
District 5 Total	87	77	297	303	139	120	523	500
Indiana	2	2	103	104	70	55	175	161
Michigan	...	1	38	35	27	28	65	64
District 6 Total	2	3	141	139	97	83	240	225
Illinois	75	73	139	155	259	211	473	439
Wisconsin	...	0	43	35	93	84	136	119
District 7 Total	75	73	182	190	352	295	609	558

*As of 31 Dec.

Continued

Table 14 (Continued)

State	State Stock 1968*	1974*	Federal 1968*	1974*	State Mutual 1968*	1974*	Total 1968*	1974*
Iowa	...	...	44	44	36	32	80	76
Minnesota	...	...	53	48	11	10	64	58
Missouri	...	...	45	42	79	74	124	116
North Dakota	...	...	7	10	4	1	11	11
South Dakota	4	5	8	9	3	2	15	16
District 8 Total	4	5	157	153	133	119	294	277
Arkansas	17	22	40	41	5	5	62	68
Louisiana	...	...	36	37	68	70	104	107
Mississippi	4	5	31	33	5	...	40	38
New Mexico	11	13	10	10	10	9	31	32
Texas	159	187	84	75	23	33	266	295
District 9 Total	191	227	201	196	111	117	503	540
Colorado	23	17	20	19	12	11	55	47
Kansas	39	36	29	30	21	21	89	87
Nebraska	...	...	21	24	20	15	41	39
Oklahoma	...	...	30	30	22	21	52	51
District 10 Total	62	53	100	103	75	68	237	224
Arizona	11	11	2	4	...	...	13	15
California	177	87	71	79	9	9	257	175
Nevada	5	6	1	1	...	0	6	7
District 11 Total	193	104	74	84	9	9	276	197
Alaska	...	...	3	4	...	...	3	4
Hawaii	3	1	2	5	5	2	10	8
Idaho	3	3	8	8	...	...	11	11
Montana	...	...	9	11	3	1	12	12
Oregon	11	9	18	17	1	1	30	27
Utah	6	4	6	5	3	3	15	12
Washington	17	12	35	30	13	8	65	50
Wyoming	3	4	9	9	...	...	12	13
Guam	1	2	...	...	...	...	1	2
District 12 Total	44	35	90	89	25	15	159	139

*As of 31 Dec.

merger rate of 14.3 percent.[8] Thus, of the three types of S&Ls, state mutuals were least able to compensate for the decline in number caused by merger.[9]

Implications

First, because of the more liberal merger policy in terms of denial rate and the FHLBB's use of merging and branching powers, many believe that federally chartered S&Ls were able to merge at a more rapid rate during 1969 through 1974 than in any previous period. Tables 5 through 10 show that federal S&Ls were the dominant acquisition institutions for the savings and loan industry in every year during the period except 1969. They were especially dominant in 1973 and 1974, conducting well over one-half of the acquisitions.

Second, the number of state mutual S&Ls declined appreciably through acquisition in the years 1969 through 1974. FHLBB officials have expressed the view that during that period there was an informal effort to eliminate very small and marginally successful S&Ls, a high proportion of which were state mutual S&Ls. Pennsylvania, New Jersey, and Illinois felt the major effect of this policy, losing through merger 49, 32, and 31 state mutual S&Ls respectively. (See Table 15.)

The relative decline in state mutual associations decreases the balance in the present dual system of regulation of savings and loans.[10] Thus, contrary to the commercial banking industry's tendency toward state regulation,[11] in the savings and loan industry the tendency is toward federal regulation. In terms of this study, the tendency is reflected and aided by the mergers which have occured during the 1969-1974 period.

Third, state stock S&Ls have maintained their rather vigorous rates of merger both in acquiring and acquired roles, although they were not as predominant in this area during the last two years of the study as they had been earlier. To a significant extent this situation results from the decline in mergers of state stock S&Ls in California. To illustrate: During 1973 and 1974, California stock S&Ls made 14 acquisitions and 9 California stock associations were acquired. By contrast, in the earlier period 1969-72, these numbers had been 62 and 69, respectively. The regulators of the savings and loan industry in California have expressed concern regarding the anti-competitive effects of mergers by associations in California, which I feel has brought about this decrease.

Asset Size Comparisons

Findings

During the 1969-1974 period, acquired associations were concentrated in the classes of small asset size. As Table 4 shows, 73 percent of the acquired associations had assets of less than $25 million, and 51 percent had assets of less than $10 million. This relationship remained stable over 1969 through 1974, as Tables 5 through 10 demonstrate. The major difference between the asset size relationship found during the period and that of previous periods occurs in the size distribution of the acquiring associations. Thirty-two percent of the acquiring associations had over $200 million in assets. This percentage compares to the 12.5 percent in the same size category for 1958 to 1967, as presented by Brigham and Pettit.[12] It appears that the larger associations have found it more desirable than have smaller associations to expand through merger as well as through branching. This conclusion is reinforced by the relatively low merger denial rate described above.

As would be expected, acquiring associations tended to be larger than the acquired associations. Overall, the acquiring association was smaller than the acquired association in 30 cases and larger in 480 cases. In most of the 30 cases in which the acquiring association was smaller, the acquired association had the more desirable type of charter or lending limit.

The third exhibit in Table 4 compares median asset size for each type of merger that occurred from 1969 through 1974. Tables 5 through 10 show the corresponding comparison for each year in this period. State mutual S&L acquisitions were of S&Ls in the smallest asset size category, while stock S&L mergers acquired S&Ls of the largest asset size. Thus, the relative increase in asset size by acquiring S&Ls can be traced to mergers in which the acquiring S&L was a federal or state stock S&L. For reasons discussed above, the increase in acquisitions by federal S&Ls is probably a result of Board policy in the last few years.

Implications

If the relative size of the acquiring S&L is an important factor in reducing competition, the tendency which is manifested in mergers of savings and loan associations, then acquisitions by state mutuals appear to offer less cause for concern about suppressed competition that do other types of mergers. Of course, this conclusion, which is based on the relatively small size of those S&Ls, may not be accurate in all cases, since it is the percentage of the market (lending and deposit) held by the association which is the key factor in this context, and total assets size may not perfectly reflect this percentage. Major areas of concern about

Table 15
ANALYSIS OF MERGERS, BY AREA, 1969 - 1974

Area	Type of Acquisition									Total Mergers	Merger Rate
	Federal Association by Federal Association	Stock Association by Federal Association	State Mutual Association by Federal Association	Federal Association by Stock Association	Stock Association by Stock Association	State Mutual Association by Stock Association	Federal Association by State Mutual Association	Stock Association by State Mutual Association	State Mutual Association by State Mutual Association		
Connecticut	...	...	2	...	...	...	...	...	1	3	8.1
Maine	...	...	3	...	...	...	1	...	...	4	16.3
Massachusetts	2	...	...	...	...	...	...	...	...	2	5.6
New Hampshire	...	...	...	...	...	...	...	...	...	...	...
Rhode Island	...	...	1	...	...	...	...	...	...	1	14.2
Vermont	...	...	...	...	...	...	...	...	1	1	13.3
District 1 Total	*2*		*6*				*1*		*2*	*11*	*8.4*
New Jersey	2	...	7	...	...	...	3	...	25	37	18.0
New York	2	...	9	...	...	...	1	...	15	27	15.4
Puerto Rico	1	...	...	...	...	...	...	...	...	1	10.0
Virgin Islands	...	...	...	...	...	...	...	...	...	...	...
District 2 Total	*5*		*16*				*4*		*40*	*65*	*16.7*
Delaware	...	...	...	...	...	...	...	...	...	...	...
Pennsylvania	14	...	22	...	...	...	7	...	27	70	23.4
West Virginia	...	...	...	...	...	...	...	...	1	1	3.3
District 3 Total	*14*		*22*				*7*		*28*	*71*	*21.4*
Alabama	4	...	1	...	...	...	...	...	...	5	8.4
Dist. of Co.	2	...	4	...	...	...	...	...	...	6	20.1
Florida	17	...	1	...	...	...	...	...	...	18	13.5
Georgia	10	...	2	...	...	...	...	...	...	12	11.8
Maryland	7	...	3	...	...	...	...	...	...	10	12.2
North Carolina	...	...	...	...	...	...	...	...	5	5	3.0
South Carolina	...	...	...	...	...	...	...	...	2	2	2.8
Virginia	3	1	...	...	3	...	1	...	...	8	5.7
District 4 Total	*43*	*1*	*11*		*3*		*1*		*7*	*66*	*9.4*
Kentucky	5	...	...	...	...	...	...	...	...	5	4.8
Ohio	5	5	6	...	7	...	1	...	13	37	11.1
Tennessee	3	...	...	...	...	...	...	...	...	3	4.1
District 5 Total	*13*	*5*	*6*		*7*		*1*		*13*	*45*	*8.8*

State							No.	%
Indiana	3		8	1		2	14	8.3
Michigan	2		1			1	4	6.2
District 6 Total	*5*		*9*	*1*		*3*	*18*	*7.7*
Illinois	9		10	2	5	21	47	10.3
Wisconsin	2		6	3		9	20	15.6
District 7 Total	*11*		*16*	*5*	*5*	*30*	*67*	*11.5*
Iowa	2		2			1	5	6.4
Minnesota	5					1	6	9.8
Missouri	5		3	1		4	13	0.8
North Dakota								
South Dakota								
District 8 Total	*12*		*5*	*1*		*6*	*24*	*8.4*
Arkansas				1			1	1.5
Louisiana								
Mississippi	1					1	2	5.1
New Mexico				1			1	3.2
Texas	2		1				3	1.0
District 9 Total	*3*		*1*	*2*		*1*	*7*	*1.3*
Colorado	1		1		7		9	17.6
Kansas					5		5	5.6
Nebraska	1		2				3	7.5
Oklahoma	1		1				2	3.9
District 10 Total	*3*		*4*		*12*		*19*	*8.4*
Arizona			1				1	
California	8		12		75		95	44.4
Nevada								
District 11 Total	*8*		*13*		*75*		*96*	*40.6*
Alaska								
Hawaii								
Idaho								
Montana								
Oregon	2	4					6	21.1
Utah	1			2			3	22.2
Washington	3	1			7		11	19.1
Wyoming				1			1	8.0
Guam								
District 12 Total	*6*	*5*		*3*	*7*		*21*	*14.1*

Source:- Federal Home Loan Bank Board.

anticompetitive tendencies appear to be acquisitions of federal S&Ls and stock S&Ls by federal S&Ls and also acquisitions of stock S&Ls by stock S&Ls.

It is interesting that these comparisions showed acquisitions of stock associations by federal S&Ls involved, as acquiring partners, the associations with largest median assets. Federal associations will be permitted to convert from mutual ownership to stock ownership in the near future (this is presently being done to a limited extent), however, and more acquisitions of stock S&Ls are expected to occur. Thus, a change in this asset size relationship is likely.

Branching Restriction and Merger Rates

Table 15 shows the total merger rate for each state and FHLB District for 31 December 1968, through 31 December 1974. For the purposes of this study, we want to determine the effect which the degree of branching restriction, as it varied between states as of year-end 1968, had on the merger rates of S&Ls in 1968 through 1974. If an S&L cannot establish as a branch the office of an S&L that it acquires, then much of the incentive to merge (obtaining the additional location and deposits) is lost. It is hypothesized that because of the merger policy followed by the FHLBB from 1969 through 1974 (see note 6), the degree of branching restriction in 1968 was not a significant variable in affecting the state merger rates in 1969-1974.

Although it is difficult to specify a perfect measure of the relative degree of branching restrictions among states, a useful measure is the average number of branches per S&L per state.[13] The average number of branches per S&L per state at 30 September 1968 and 30 September 1974 are shown in Table 16. The relationship between the degree of branching restriction and the rate of merger activity will be tested by determining the rank correlation between the statewide merger rate for 1969-74 and the average number of branches per S&L in each state as of year-end 1968.[14] The nonparametric rank correlation test is appropriate in this situation, because it is more likely that a state with four offices per S&L is less restrictive about branching than another state with one office per S&L than that the reverse is the case. The Spearman rank correlation between the degree of state branching restriction and the degree of merger activity for 1969-74 is 0.34, which is statistically significant at less than the 0.01 level. If the degree of branching restriction were the completely dominant factor in effecting merger rates among states, the rank correlation coefficient would be 1.0. From this we must conclude that state branching restrictions have been significant but not dominant in affecting the rate of merger. Savings and loan associations have been able and willing to merge even in states where branching restrictions have been relatively stringent. This conclusion is consistent with the merger policy of the FHLBB as described above.

Table 16
AVERAGE BRANCHES PER ASSOCIATION,
FSLIC-INSURED ASSOCIATIONS

Location	30 Sept. 1968	30 Sept. 1974	Increase
Connecticut	2.08	3.31	1.23
Maine	1.19	1.62	0.43
Massachusetts	1.26	2.83	1.59
New Hampshire	1.00	1.00	...
Rhode Island	2.88	5.00	2.12
Vermont	1.00	1.29	0.29
District 1 Total	1.39	2.51	1.12
New Jersey	1.76	3.02	1.26
New York	2.04	3.47	1.43
Puerto Rico	2.56	5.27	2.71
Virgin Islands	2.00	2.00	...
District 2 Total	1.91	3.29	1.38
Delaware	1.00	2.75	1.75
Pennsylvania	1.49	2.48	0.99
West Virginia	1.00	1.30	0.30
District 3 Total	1.35	2.37	1.02
Alabama	1.67	2.86	1.19
Dist. of Col.	2.40	3.75	1.35
Florida	2.15	4.73	2.58
Georgia	1.59	3.13	1.54
Maryland	1.76	2.83	1.07
North Carolina	1.58	2.15	0.57
South Carolina	1.67	2.38	0.71
Virginia	2.23	3.94	1.71
District 4 Total	1.83	3.20	1.37
Kentucky	1.27	1.58	0.31
Ohio	1.73	2.79	1.06
Tennessee	1.54	2.13	0.59
District 5 Total	1.63	2.44	1.40
Indiana	1.37	1.78	0.41
Michigan	3.43	5.63	2.20
District 6 Total	1.93	2.87	0.94
Illinois	1.00	1.31	0.31
Wisconsin	1.16	2.45	1.29
District 7 Total	1.03	1.55	0.52

Continued

Table 16 (Continued)

Location	30 Sept. 1968	30 Sept. 1974	Increase
Iowa	1.18	2.12	0.94
Minnesota	1.72	3.24	1.52
Missouri	1.71	2.97	1.26
North Dakota	2.00	4.18	2.18
South Dakota	1.06	1.19	0.13
District 8 Total	1.54	2.74	1.20
Arkansas	1.19	1.85	0.66
Louisiana	1.22	1.93	0.71
Mississippi	1.15	2.05	0.90
New Mexico	1.45	2.09	0.64
Texas	1.69	2.72	1.03
District 9 Total	1.47	2.37	0.90
Colorado	2.36	4.28	1.92
Kansas	1.53	2.16	0.63
Nebraska	1.49	2.55	1.06
Oklahoma	1.45	2.31	0.86
District 10 Total	1.69	2.71	1.02
Arizona	5.31	10.60	5.29
California	3.08	8.68	5.60
Nevada	4.00	5.71	1.71
District 11 Total	3.20	8.72	5.52
Alaska	1.67	3.75	2.08
Hawaii	4.33	8.80	4.47
Idaho	2.50	3.00	0.50
Montana	1.36	1.85	0.49
Oregon	2.97	6.34	3.37
Utah	2.07	3.08	1.01
Washington	2.30	4.71	2.41
Wyoming	1.15	1.54	0.39
Guam	1.00	1.50	0.50
District 12 Total	2.52	4.72	2.20

Source: Federal Home Loan Bank Board.

Another interesting relationship is the association between the change in number of branches per association and the merger rate of associations. The change in the number of branches per S&L in each state from 30 September 1968 to 30 September 1974 is shown in column 3 of Table 16. It is informative to determine the effect that merging has had on the increase in the average number of branches per association among the states. The coefficient of correlation between the state merger rate for 1969-74 and the increase in the average number of branches was calculated and found to be 0.46. This means that 21 percent of the change in branches per association can be explained by the relationship between branching and merger.

NOTES

1. James Gillies and Frank Mittlebach, *Mergers of Savings and Loan Associations in California* (Los Angeles: University of California, 1959).

2. Eugene F. Brigham and R. Richardson Pettit, "Effects of Structure on Performance of the Savings and Loan Industry," in *Study of the Savings and Loan Industry*, ed. by Irwin Friend (Washington, D.C.: Government Printing Office, 1969).

3. *Ibid.*, p. 1047.

4. *Ibid.*, p. 1083.

5. *Ibid.*, p. 1070.

6. According to J.G. Harth, "One state, Florida, prohibited branching for all state financial institutions, but the banks avoided the prohibition by means of a device called chain banking; consequently FHLBB revised its policy to allow federal association branches in states where chain or affiliate banking was carried on. The prohibitory Florida savings and loan statute later was repealed, and savings and loan branching is now authorized in that state." See "Additional Offices and Facilities of Savings and Loan Associations," *Legal Bulletin* (U.S. League of Savings Associations), May 1974.

7. The Mann-Whitney U test utilizes relative rankings of the samples concerned to test for stochastic differences between the underlying distribution functions of the samples' populations. Briefly, the merger rate of each type of association is computed for each year. The value of U (the statistic used in this test) is determined by the number of times that the merger rate for one group (e.g., state stock associations) is greater than the merger rate for the comparison group (e.g., federals). The sampling distribution of U is known, and for a one-tailed test we can determine the probability associated with the occurrence under the null hypothesis of any U value as extreme as an observed value of U. See S. Siegel, *Nonparametric Statistics* (New York: McGraw-Hill, 1956), pp. 116-26.

8. These merger rates refer to the rates at which the associations were acquired.

9. Disappearances through merger are typically offset by the chartering of new associations. They are much less commonly offset by conversion from one type of association to another type (e.g., state stock to state mutual).

10. On a net basis, 103 state S&Ls came under federal regulation through merger. Seventy-eight of those S&Ls were state mutuals.

11. See F. Knight,"Comparative Reserve Requirements at Member and Nonmember Banks," *Monthly Review,* April 1974.

12. Brigham and Pettit, "Effects of Structure...," p. 1054.

13. The average number of branches per S&L generally parallels the degree of branching restriction in each state during the period as described in J.G. Harth "Additional Offices...." Discussions with FHLB officials also corroborated this relationship.

14. For these tests, Guam, Puerto Rico, Hawaii, Alaska, and the Virgin Islands were not included because of their unique geographic and/or political characteristics.

III

FINANCIAL COMPARISONS OF ACQUIRING ASSOCIATIONS

The data discussed in the financial comparisons were gathered from quarterly and semi-annual financial reports of the relevant S&Ls which were stored in the computer files of the Federal Home Loan Bank Board. The Board extensively changed its financial reporting forms in 1971, so, for the purpose of continuity, the analysis will be confined primarily to those financial data which are available for the entire 1969-74 period.

One criticism of earlier studies comparing acquired and acquiring firms is that they have aggregated the financial comparisons over time. The critics believe that, in doing so, the analyses may ignore time trends of relationships, and hence one uniquely different subperiod may so dominate the results over the aggregate period that incorrect conclusions may result. In attempting to minimize this effect, our analysis will examine data for both the aggregate period (Table 17) and also for each year individually (Tables 18-23).

General Hypotheses

The existing literature on merger theory and policy suggests many reasons for which one firm acquires another. A number of authors maintain that the possibilities of operating economies is the only justification for a merger when the objective of the firm is to maximize the owners' wealth.[1]

In a practical sense, however, S&Ls may have less-involved reasons for merging. Brigham and Pettit found that the top four reasons for merging given by acquiring S&Ls were to:

1. Become larger (able to make larger loans and improve service to the area)
2. Gain a new branch with trained personnel at low cost
3. Grow or obtain a location for growth in a growing community
4. Gain additional strength through increased size and additional reserves [2]

37

Table 17

FINANCIAL RATIO COMPARISON
FOR MERGED SAVINGS AND LOAN ASSOCIATIONS,
AGGREGATE ANALYSIS, 1969-74
(N = 510)

	Acquiring Association	Acquired Association	t Ratio
Asset Structure			
Single family mortgages/ total mortgages	75.98 (13.9)	79.73 (16.6)	−4.85***
FHA and VA mortgages/ total mortgages	12.46 (15.2)	6.07 (12.5)	8.60***
Average conventional mortgage size (in $ thousands)	16.92 (6.1)	14.19 (6.3)	8.67***
Overall average mortgage size (in $ thousands)	16.08 (5.5)	14.15 (6.6)	6.32***
Total mortgages/ total assets	84.16 (7.2)	83.72 (7.4)	1.02
Cash plus demand deposits/ total assets	1.41 (1.8)	2.87 (3.0)	−10.34***
Investments plus other liquid assets/ total assets	7.76 (3.7)	8.14 (4.8)	−1.64*
Fixed assets/ total assets	1.52 (1.5)	1.24 (1.2)	3.29***
Real estate owned and in judgment/ total assets	0.33 (0.9)	0.45 (1.0)	−2.10**
Nonconforming loans and contracts/facilitate sales of REO to total mortgages	0.62 (2.2)	0.59 (1.6)	0.30
Liability Structure			
FHLBB advances/ total assets	5.62 (5.8)	3.99 (5.2)	6.19***
Borrowings other than from FHLBB/ total assets	0.59 (1.4)	0.56 (1.5)	0.29
Total deposits/ total assets	83.51 (5.9)	85.54 (7.4)	−5.55***
Proportion of depositors with accounts above insured limit	1.42 (1.0)	1.14 (0.9)	6.09***
Average deposit account size	3.41 (1.0)	3.09 (1.0)	5.43***
Net worth/total assets	6.87 (2.7)	6.97 (2.9)	−0.65

Continued

Table 17 (Continued)
(N = 510)

	Acquiring Association	Acquired Association	t Ratio
Income Structure			
Interest income on mortgages/ total mortgages	6.44 (1.1)	6.51 (0.7)	−1.41*
Interest income on mortgages/ gross income	83.41 (4.2)	83.96 (7.0)	−1.71**
Operating income/ total assets	6.48 (1.4)	6.39 (0.6)	1.52*
Income before tax/ total assets	0.94 (1.5)	0.60 (0.7)	4.78***
Net income/gross income	10.10 (4.2)	7.21 (10.0)	6.22***
Net income/net worth	10.31 (5.1)	6.36 (14.4)	6.00***
Net income/total assets	0.73 (1.3)	0.48 (0.6)	4.14***
Cost Structure			
Personnel compensation plus directors' fees/ operating expenses	47.60 (6.5)	50.30 (9.9)	−5.92***
Personnel compensation plus directors' fees/ total deposits	0.65 (0.2)	0.77 (0.3)	−8.47***
Advertising expenses/ operating expenses	9.78 (4.3)	6.41 (4.8)	13.39***
Advertising expenses/ total deposits	0.14 (0.1)	0.10 (0.1)	7.04***
Occupancy expenses/ operating expenses	11.43 (5.0)	10.90 (6.5)	1.55*
Occupancy expenses/ total assets	0.14 (0.1)	0.15 (0.1)	−1.54*
Deposit interest (dividends)/ operating income	63.73 (6.1)	64.80 (7.2)	−3.29***
Deposit interest (dividends)/ total deposits	4.99 (1.4)	4.88 (0.6)	1.80**
Operating expenses/ operating income	17.64 (3.8)	20.41 (7.3)	−8.41***

NOTE: The number on the left represents the mean, and the number in parentheses represents the standard deviation. All numbers are percentages unless otherwise stated.
*Significant at the 0.10 level (one-tailed test).
**Significant at the 0.05 level (one-tailed test).
***Significant at the 0.01 level (one-tailed test).

Table 18
FINANCIAL RATIO COMPARISON
FOR MERGED SAVINGS AND LOAN ASSOCIATIONS, 1969
(N=47)

	Acquiring Association	Acquired Association	*t* Ratio
Asset Structure			
Single family mortgages/ total mortgages	74.97 (16.6)	78.83 (17.0)	−1.74**
FHA and VA mortgages/ total mortgages	5.96 (11.1)	1.92 (4.9)	2.61***
Average conventional mortgage size (in $ thousands)	14.94 (6.6)	12.47 (5.7)	3.19***
Overall average mortgage size (in $ thousands)	14.63 (6.2)	12.37 (5.6)	3.07***
Total mortgages/ total assets	85.9 (2.8)	85.2 (3.2)	0.98
Cash plus demand deposits/ total assets	1.76 (2.2)	3.25 (2.9)	−4.16***
Investments plus other liquid assets/ total assets	7.07 (2.1)	5.61 (3.3)	3.06***
Fixed assets/ total assets	1.42(1.1)	1.10 (1.0)	1.42*
Real estate owned and in judgment/ total assets	0.58 (1.7)	0.83 (1.1)	−0.88
Nonconforming loans and contracts to facilitate sales of REO/ total mortgages	0.80 (1.4)	1.35 (2.7)	−1.54*
Liability Structure			
FHLBB advances/ total assets	4.70 (4.2)	4.20 (5.7)	0.56
Borrowings other than from FHLBB/ total assets	0.44 (1.2)	0.44 (1.7)	0.00
Total deposits/ total assets	85.31 (4.9)	85.50 (9.9)	0.12
Proportion of depositors with accounts above insured limit	1.76 (1.0)	1.50 (1.1)	1.43*
Average deposit account size (in $ thousands)	3.02 (0.8)	2.66 (0.9)	2.77***
Net worth/total assets	7.40 (1.5)	7.18 (2.6)	0.54

Continued

Table 18 (Continued)
(N = 47)

	Acquiring Association	Acquired Association	*t* Ratio
Income Structure			
Interest income on mortgages/ total mortgages	5.95 (0.4)	6.10 (0.8)	−1.14
Interest income on mortgages/ gross income	84.83 (3.6)	84.53 (8.0)	0.24
Operating income/ total assets	5.97 (0.4)	6.04 (0.6)	−1.04
Income before tax/ total assets	0.76 (0.3)	0.62 (0.5)	1.83**
Net income/gross income	10.55 (3.6)	8.31 (7.9)	1.80**
Net income/net worth	9.00 (4.0)	8.11 (6.4)	0.24
Net income/total assets	0.64 (0.2)	0.53 (0.5)	1.49*
Cost Structure			
Personnel compensation plus directors' fees/ operating expenses	46.10 (7.2)	46.46 (7.1)	−0.31
Personnel compensation plus directors' fees/ total deposits	0.60 (0.2)	0.74 (0.3)	−3.22***
Advertising expenses/ operating expenses	9.48 (4.0)	6.42 (4.1)	4.32***
Advertising expenses/ total deposits	0.12 (0.1)	0.10 (0.1)	1.24
Occupancy expenses/ operating expenses	13.08 (6.7)	12.09 (6.1)	0.80
Occupancy expenses/ total assets	0.15 (0.1)	0.16 (0.1)	−0.94
Deposit interest (dividends)/ operating income	64.86 (4.5)	64.08 (7.1)	0.76
Deposit interest (dividends)/ total deposits	4.53 (0.3)	4.64 (1.3)	−0.61
Operating expenses/ operating income	18.72 (3.8)	22.67 (9.2)	−2.89***

NOTE: The number on the left represents the mean and the number in parentheses represents the standard deviation. All numbers are percentages unless otherwise stated.
*Significant at the 0.10 level (one-tailed test).
**Significant at the 0.05 level (one-tailed test).
***Significant at the 0.01 level (one-tailed test).

Table 19
FINANCIAL RATIO COMPARISON
FOR MERGED SAVINGS AND LOAN ASSOCIATIONS, 1970
(N=78)

	Acquiring Association	Acquired Association	*t* Ratio
Asset Structure			
Single family mortgages/ total mortgages	74.77 (15.9)	77.29 (16.6)	−1.19
FHA and VA mortgages/ total mortgages	10.92 (1.4)	5.95 (16.0)	3.10***
Average conventional mortgage size (in $ thousands)	14.30 (4.9)	12.24 (4.6)	3.80***
Overall average mortgage size (in $ thousands)	13.91 (4.4)	12.17 (4.6)	3.75***
Total mortgages/ total assets	87.63 (2.5)	87.02 (2.9)	1.36*
Cash plus demand deposits/ total assets	1.31 (1.4)	2.61 (2.5)	−4.51***
Investments plus other liquid assets/ total assets	6.15 (1.8)	5.34 (2.4)	2.34***
Fixed assets/ total assets	1.62 (1.0)	1.36 (1.4)	1.32*
Real estate owned and in judgment/ total assets	0.43 (1.2)	0.47 (0.9)	−0.20
Nonconforming loans and contracts to facilitate sales of REO/ total mortgages	0.67 (1.9)	0.58 (0.9)	0.43
Liability Structure			
FHLBB advances/ total assets	7.15 (5.6)	5.56 (5.7)	2.29**
Borrowings other than from FHLBB/ total assets	0.25 (0.7)	0.45 (1.1)	−1.60*
Total deposits/ total assets	82.36 (5.4)	84.06 (6.0)	−2.57***
Proportion of depositors with accounts above insured limit	0.64 (0.7)	0.52 (0.6)	1.23
Average deposit account size (in $ thousands)	3.12 (1.6)	2.74 (0.9)	1.80**
Net worth/total assets	7.72 (3.1)	7.50 (2.5)	0.56

Continued

Table 19 (Continued)
(N=78)

	Acquiring Association	Acquired Association	*t* Ratio
Income Structure			
Interest income on mortgages/ total mortgages	5.98 (0.5)	6.23 (0.5)	−4.38***
Interest income on mortgages/ gross income	85.58 (2.9)	87.02 (3.6)	−2.99***
Operating income/ total assets	6.06 (0.4)	6.20 (0.5)	−3.09***
Income before tax/ total assets	0.77 (0.4)	0.58 (0.4)	3.08***
Net income/gross income	10.53 (5.3)	7.96 (5.8)	2.81***
Net income/net worth	9.23 (5.9)	7.38 (7.8)	1.66*
Net income/total assets	0.64 (0.3)	0.50 (0.4)	2.50***
Cost Structure			
Personnel compensation plus directors' fees/ operating expenses	47.20 (2.9)	49.22 (7.8)	−1.92**
Personnel compensation plus directors' fees/ total deposits	0.65 (0.1)	0.77 (0.2)	−5.14***
Advertising expenses/ operating expenses	10.29 (4.5)	6.43 (4.0)	5.96***
Advertising expenses/ total deposits	0.15 (0.1)	0.10 (0.1)	4.38***
Occupancy expenses/ operating expenses	11.64 (5.0)	11.95 (6.9)	−0.34
Occupancy expenses/ total assets	0.13 (0.1)	0.16 (0.1)	−1.81**
Deposit interest (dividends)/ operating income	63.43 (6.3)	64.66 (5.0)	−1.56*
Deposit interest (dividends)/ total deposits	4.67 (0.5)	4.76 (0.3)	−1.88**
Operating expenses/ operating income	18.72 (3.2)	21.32 (4.8)	−4.38***

NOTE: The number on the left represents the mean and the number in parentheses represents the standard deviation. All numbers are percentages unless otherwise stated.
*Significant at the 0.10 level (one-tailed test).
**Significant at the 0.05 level (one-tailed test).
***Significant at the 0.01 level (one-tailed test).

Table 20
FINANCIAL RATIO COMPARISON
FOR MERGED SAVINGS AND LOAN ASSOCIATIONS, 1971
(N = 116)

	Acquiring Association	Acquired Association	*t* Ratio
Asset Structure			
Single family mortgages/ total mortgages	76.14 (14.8)	79.38 (18.9)	−1.72**
FHA and VA mortgages/ total mortgages	13.08 (17.0)	5.69 (12.2)	4.41***
Average conventional mortgage size (in $ thousands)	14.91 (5.0)	12.14 (5.0)	5.04***
Overall average mortgage size (in $ thousands)	14.27 (4.6)	11.99 (4.9)	4.36***
Total mortgages/ total assets	84.55 (9.5)	83.61 (9.3)	0.81
Cash plus demand deposits/ total assets	2.09 (2.5)	3.63 (3.8)	−3.72***
Investments plus other liquid assets/ total assets	8.28 (7.5)	6.80 (4.8)	1.90**
Fixed assets/ total assets	1.78 (2.2)	1.28 (1.1)	2.20**
Real estate owned and in judgment/ total assets	0.38 (1.0)	0.51 (1.1)	−1.02
Nonconforming loans and contracts to facilitate sales of REO to total mortgages	1.08 (3.9)	0.71 (2.2)	0.92
Liability Structure			
FHLBB advances/ total assets	7.84 (11.2)	4.86 (5.9)	3.20***
Borrowings other than from FHLBB/ total assets	0.58 (1.6)	0.13 (0.5)	3.04***
Total deposits/ total assets	82.41 (7.4)	83.98 (10.4)	−1.41*
Proportion of depositors with accounts above insured limit	0.82 (0.5)	0.76 (0.6)	0.83
Average deposit account size (in $ thousands)	2.96 (0.7)	2.77 (0.9)	1.93**
Net worth to total assets	8.29 (7.7)	7.66 (3.7)	0.80

Continued

Table 20 (Continued)
(N = 116)

	Acquiring Association	Acquired Association	*t* Ratio
Income Structure			
Interest income on mortgages/ total mortgages	6.39 (1.5)	6.42 (0.8)	−0.21
Interest income on mortgages/ gross income	84.07 (3.5)	84.36 (9.4)	−0.34
Operating income/ total assets	6.68 (2.4)	6.32 (0.8)	1.66*
Income before tax/ total assets	0.88 (1.1)	0.49 (0.5)	3.39***
Net income/gross income	9.13 (5.2)	6.03 (6.6)	4.18***
Net income/net worth	8.44 (5.1)	3.86 (14.3)	3.35***
Net income/total assets	0.71 (0.9)	0.39 (0.4)	3.37***
Cost Structure			
Personnel compensation plus directors' fees/ operating expenses	46.06 (6.8)	49.75 (11.6)	−3.37***
Personnel compensation plus directors' fees/ total deposits	0.71 (0.2)	0.85 (0.4)	−3.65***
Advertising expenses/ operating expenses	9.47 (4.8)	5.80 (5.1)	6.23***
Advertising expenses/ total deposits	0.15 (0.1)	0.10 (0.1)	3.81***
Occupancy expenses/ operating expenses	12.90 (5.6)	11.15 (6.2)	2.30**
Occupancy expenses/ total assets	0.18 (0.2)	0.16 (0.1)	0.97
Deposit interest (dividends)/ operating income	62.92 (7.1)	63.67 (9.8)	0.82
Deposit interest (dividends)/ total deposits	4.90 (0.9)	4.77 (0.6)	1.49*
Operating expenses/ operating income	19.18 (3.9)	22.41 (6.7)	−4.65***

NOTE: The number on the left represents the mean and the number in parentheses represents the standard deviation. All numbers are in percentage unless otherwise stated.
*Significant at the 0.10 level (one-tailed test).
**Significant at the 0.05 level (one-tailed test).
***Significant at the 0.01 level (one-tailed test).

Table 21
FINANCIAL RATIO COMPARISON
FOR MERGED SAVINGS AND LOAN ASSOCIATIONS, 1972
(N = 83)

	Acquiring Association	Acquired Association	*t* Ratio
Asset Structure			
Single family mortgages/ total mortgages	74.13 (11.6)	75.93 (15.4)	−1.12
FHA and VA mortgages/ total mortgages	12.25 (13.5)	5.54 (7.9)	4.13***
Average conventional mortgage size (in $ thousands)	20.76 (6.5)	19.80 (4.9)	0.77
Overall average mortgage size (in $ thousands)	22.28 (7.4)	20.50 (4.7)	1.23
Total mortgages/ total assets	85.97 (3.5)	83.66 (5.0)	3.50***
Cash plus demand deposits/ total assets	1.33 (1.6)	2.21 (2.5)	−2.94***
Investments plus other liquid assets/ total assets	9.08 (3.5)	11.25 (4.8)	−3.71***
Fixed assets/ total assets	1.27 (0.6)	1.45 (1.6)	−1.07
Real estate owned and in judgment/ total assets	0.28 (0.4)	0.47 (1.0)	1.66*
Nonconforming loans and contracts to facilitate sales of REO/ total mortgages	0.68 (1.1)	0.78 (1.8)	−0.47
Liability Structure			
FHLBB advances/ total assets	4.43 (4.8)	2.84 (4.3)	2.47***
Borrowings other than from FHLBB/ total assets	0.62 (1.4)	0.51 (1.3)	0.53
Total deposits/ total assets	83.59 (5.2)	86.93 (4.9)	−5.23***
Proportion of depositors with accounts above insured limit	2.62 (10.8)	1.10 (0.7)	1.28
Average deposit account size (in $ thousands)	3.54 (6.7)	3.20 (0.9)	3.39***
Net worth/total assets	6.64 (1.5)	6.51 (2.3)	0.49

Continued

Table 21 (Continued)
(N = 83)

	Acquiring Association	Acquired Association	*t* Ratio
Income Structure			
Interest income on mortgages/ total mortgages	6.18 (0.5)	6.36 (0.5)	−3.39***
Interest income on mortgages/ gross income	81.63 (4.7)	82.18 (5.5)	−0.84
Operating income/ total assets	6.40 (0.5)	6.35 (0.6)	0.87
Income before tax/ total assets	0.94 (0.4)	0.59 (1.1)	2.93***
Net income/gross income	10.69 (3.6)	6.37 (17.4)	2.29***
Net income/net worth	11.01 (4.6)	5.98 (19.1)	2.39***
Net income/total assets	0.70 (0.3)	0.43 (1.0)	2.42***
Cost Structure			
Personnel compensation plus directors' fees/ operating expenses	48.46 (7.0)	51.12 (10.8)	−2.37***
Personnel compensation plus directors' fees/ total deposits	0.63 (0.2)	0.69 (0.2)	−2.26**
Advertising expenses/ operating expenses	9.30 (4.4)	6.45 (4.5)	4.84***
Advertising expenses/ total deposits	0.13 (0.1)	0.09 (0.1)	3.38***
Occupancy expenses/ operating expenses	11.47 (4.1)	10.91 (5.0)	0.82
Occupancy expenses/ total assets	0.13 (0.1)	0.14 (0.1)	−0.95
Deposit interest (dividends)/ operating income	62.74 (7.0)	64.95 (6.9)	−3.28***
Deposit interest (dividends)/ total deposits	4.86 (0.2)	4.81 (0.2)	1.51*
Operating expenses/ operating income	16.65 (4.0)	18.55 (8.7)	−2.01**

NOTE: The number on the left represents the mean, and the number in parentheses represents the standard deviation. All numbers are in percentages unless otherwise stated.
*Significant at the 0.10 level (one-tailed test).
**Significant at the 0.05 level (one-tailed test).
***Significant at the 0.01 level (one-tailed test).

Table 22
FINANCIAL RATIO COMPARISON
FOR MERGED SAVINGS AND LOAN ASSOCIATIONS, 1973
(N = 69)

	Acquiring Association	Acquired Association	*t* Ratio
Asset Structure			
Single family mortgages/ total mortgages	75.43 (11.7)	79.73 (14.0)	−2.44***
FHA and VA mortgages/ total mortgages	15.39 (13.7)	6.27 (8.8)	5.47***
Average conventional mortgage size (in $ thousands)	21.03 (9.6)	19.29 (5.2)	2.11**
Overall average mortgage size (in $ thousands)	22.80 (11.7)	19.09 (4.8)	2.31**
Total mortgages/ total assets	84.46 (4.0)	83.52 (7.1)	0.95
Cash plus demand deposits/ total assets	1.07 (1.1)	3.29 (2.9)	−6.67***
Investments plus other liquid assets/ total assets	9.08 (3.3)	10.72 (4.6)	−2.56***
Fixed assets/total assets	1.42 (0.7)	0.93 (0.9)	3.42***
Real estate owned and in judgment/ total assets	0.27 (0.5)	0.44 (1.3)	−1.09
Nonconforming loans and contracts to facilitate sales of REO/ total mortgages	0.24 (0.5)	0.28 (0.6)	−0.61
Liability Structure			
FHLBB advances/ total assets	4.21 (4.5)	2.45 (3.8)	3.16***
Borrowings other than from FHLBB/ total assets	0.62 (1.3)	0.75 (1.9)	−0.47
Total deposits/ total assets	84.50 (5.3)	87.13 (4.8)	−3.87***
Proportion of depositors with accounts above insured limit	1.75 (1.1)	1.37 (0.9)	2.54***
Average deposit account size (in $ thousands)	3.62 (0.7)	3.22 (0.8)	3.31***
Net worth/total assets	5.99 (1.5)	6.87 (2.7)	−2.60***

Continued

Table 22 (Continued)
(N = 69)

	Acquiring Association	Acquired Association	*t* Ratio
Income Structure			
Interest income on mortgages/ total mortgages	6.21 (0.3)	6.50 (0.5)	−4.97***
Interest income on mortgages/ gross income	82.03 (4.6)	84.37 (5.9)	−2.82***
Operating income/ total assets	6.31 (0.3)	6.32 (0.4)	−0.21
Income before tax/ total assets	0.86 (0.3)	0.61 (0.7)	3.40***
Net income/gross income	9.92 (3.3)	6.85 (12.7)	2.07***
Net income/net worth	11.15 (4.2)	6.18 (16.7)	2.49***
Net income/total assets	0.64 (0.2)	0.46 (0.8)	1.97**
Cost Structure			
Personnel compensation plus directors' fees/ operating expenses	49.64 (6.1)	54.05 (11.7)	−3.06***
Personnel compensation plus directors' fees/ total deposits	0.63 (0.2)	0.73 (0.3)	−2.97***
Advertising expenses/ operating expenses	9.72 (3.8)	5.72 (5.7)	5.62***
Advertising expenses/ total deposits	0.13 (0.1)	0.08 (0.1)	3.45***
Occupancy expenses/ operating expenses	9.94 (3.6)	10.25 (9.7)	−0.25
Occupancy expenses/ total assets	0.11 (0.1)	0.12 (0.1)	−1.09
Deposit interest (dividends)/ operating income	65.26 (6.0)	66.47 (6.7)	−1.48*
Deposit interest (dividends)/ total deposits	4.92 (0.2)	4.88 (0.3)	1.16
Operating expenses/ operating income	16.79 (3.6)	18.38 (5.6)	−2.30**

NOTE: The number on the left represents the mean and the number in parentheses represents the standard deviation. All numbers are in percentages unless otherwise stated.
*Significant at the 0.10 level (one-tailed test).
**Significant at the 0.05 level (one-tailed test).
***Significant at the 0.01 level (one-tailed test).

Table 23
FINANCIAL RATIO COMPARISON
FOR MERGED SAVINGS AND LOAN ASSOCIATIONS, 1974
(N = 118)

	Acquiring Association	Acquired Association	t Ratio
Asset Structure			
Single family mortgages/ total mortgages	79.37 (13.3)	84.87 (15.4)	−3.18***
FHA and VA mortgages/ total mortgages	13.73 (17.3)	8.46 (15.9)	2.64***
Average conventional mortgage size (in $ thousands)	20.17 (6.0)	15.15 (5.6)	8.64***
Overall average mortgage size (in $ thousands)	18.06 (5.2)	14.51 (5.4)	7.10***
Total mortgages/ total assets	79.28 (8.8)	81.20 (8.9)	−1.70**
Cash plus demand deposits/ total assets	0.90 (1.3)	2.38 (2.9)	−5.58***
Investments plus other liquid assets/ total assets	7.25 (3.8)	8.62 (4.5)	−2.92***
Fixed assets/ total assets	1.31 (0.7)	1.22 (1.1)	0.92
Real estate owned and in judgment/ total assets	0.19 (0.3)	0.22 (0.6)	−0.43
Nonconforming loans and contracts to facilitate sales of REO/ total mortgages	0.22 (0.5)	0.20 (0.7)	0.20
Liability Structure			
FHLBB advances/ total assets	5.14 (4.2)	3.72 (5.0)	2.96***
Borrowings other than from FHLBB/ total assets	0.85 (1.7)	1.04 (2.1)	−0.86
Total deposits/ total assets	83.76 (5.2)	86.32 (5.6)	−4.54***
Proportion of depositors with accounts above insured limit	2.19 (1.2)	1.70 (0.9)	4.44***
Average deposit account size (in $ thousands)	4.00 (1.0)	3.67 (1.2)	2.22**
Net worth/total assets	5.97 (1.6)	6.24 (2.6)	−1.07

Continued

Table 23 (Continued)
(N = 118)

	Acquiring Association	Acquired Association	*t* Ratio
Income Structure			
Interest income on mortgages/ total mortgages	7.25 (0.9)	7.04 (0.8)	1.81**
Interest income on mortgages/ gross income	82.83 (4.4)	82.39 (6.2)	0.67
Operating income/ total assets	6.80 (0.3)	6.79 (0.4)	0.26
Income before tax/ total assets	0.97 (0.3)	0.72 (0.5)	4.57***
Net income/gross income	10.20 (2.9)	8.13 (6.2)	3.23***
Net income/net worth	12.31 (4.7)	10.62 (9.1)	1.86***
Net income/total assets	0.70 (0.2)	0.56 (0.4)	3.15***
Cost Structure			
Personnel compensation plus directors' fees/ operating expenses	48.25 (5.8)	50.34 (7.9)	−2.46***
Personnel compensation plus directors' fees/ total deposits	0.64 (0.2)	0.78 (0.3)	−4.94***
Advertising expenses/ operating expenses	10.21 (3.7)	7.34 (4.8)	5.67***
Advertising expenses/ total deposits	0.14 (0.1)	0.12 (0.1)	1.64*
Occupancy expenses/ operating expenses	10.03 (4.1)	9.87 (4.8)	0.29
Occupancy expenses/ total assets	0.11 (0.1)	0.14 (0.1)	−2.23**
Deposit interest (dividends)/ operating income	64.08 (4.7)	65.34 (5.5)	−2.36***
Deposit interest (dividends)/ total deposits	5.24 (0.2)	5.21 (0.4)	1.10
Operating expenses/ operating income	16.22 (2.9)	19.46 (7.5)	−4.48***

NOTE: The number on the left represents the mean and the number in parentheses represents the standard deviation. All numbers are percentages unless otherwise stated.
*Significant at the 0.10 level (one-tailed test).
**Significant at the 0.05 level (one-tailed test).
***Significant at the 0.01 level (one-tailed test).

The top four reasons given for merging by acquired S&Ls were:

1. Weak institution, too small to compete
2. Get better management, younger personnel, improve service
3. Retiring manager, death of manager
4. Obtain benefits from combination with larger association [3]

The first reason given by the acquiring S&Ls suggests that the average mortgage loan size of the acquiring S&Ls is larger than that of the acquired S&Ls. This follows from the implicitly positive correlation between the size of the S&L and the sizes of the mortgages it finances. The fourth reason for merging given by the acquiring S&Ls suggests that other financial measures should differ between the acquiring and acquired S&Ls because of the expected greater market dominance of the acquiring S&Ls. This includes differences in liquidity and types of mortgages in the loan portfolio. The first and second reasons for merging given by the acquired S&Ls suggests that the acquiring S&Ls will be more efficient and profitable than the acquired S&Ls.

Asset Structure

Table 17 contains means, standard deviations, and *t* ratios of selected financial measures for the entire 510 regular mergers during the 1969-74 period. Tables 18 through 23 detail this information on a yearly basis. The comparisons are based on data as of the year-end preceeding the mergers.

Examination of the asset structure of S&Ls involved in merger activity during 1969 through 1974 reveals significant differences between acquiring and acquired S&Ls. With respect to the mortgage portfolio, Table 17 shows that the acquiring S&Ls had a significantly higher mean ratio of mortgages invested in financing of single-family home purchases but less invested in FHA and VA home purchases. Tables 18 through 23 show that both of these relationships were consistent each year. Likewise, the average conventional and overall mortgage size was significantly higher for acquiring S&Ls, by approximately two thousand dollars. This relationship also held consistently each year. The effect of economies of scale in the mortgage size could effect overall profitability, a question which will be investigated later. Finally, although we found that the composition of the mortgage portfolio was typically different between the acquired and acquiring S&Ls, the proportion of mortgages to total assets is found to be approximately the same for the associations.

Comparisons of liquidity measures show that the acquired S&Ls were significantly more liquid than the acquiring S&Ls. The ratio of cash plus demand deposits to total assets is significantly higher for the acquired S&Ls for both the aggregate period and individual years. The ratio of investment plus other liquid assets (excluding FHLB stock) is also significantly higher for the aggregate period, but the relationship was the opposite in 1969, 1970, and 1971. The proportion of net fixed assets to total assets was significantly higher for acquiring S&Ls in the aggregate period and for five of the six individual years.

Liability Structure

The financing patterns of acquired and acquiring associations were different in several respects. First, Federal Home Loan Bank advances were significantly higher for acquiring S&Ls. This relationship was consistent over the six-year period. Second, the ratio of total deposits to total assets was significantly lower for acquiring S&Ls, both in the aggregate period analysis and in each year. Note also that for the two types of S&Ls the proportion of the mean values of advances plus deposits to total assets is approximately equal, 89.23 percent and 89.43 percent for the acquiring and acquired S&Ls, respectively. Therefore, although the total financing from these two sources as a percentage of assets is approximately equal, the proportion of advances and deposits for acquiring and acquired S&Ls differs significantly.

Since 1971, FSLIC-insured S&Ls have been reporting in the semiannual and quarterly reports the breakdown of deposits held by type, i.e., passbook and certificate deposits.[4] Comparison of the ratio of passbook deposits to total deposits for S&Ls merging in 1972, 1973, and 1974 can give us additional insights to the differences in the financing patterns of the acquired and acquiring S&Ls. The ratios (and standard deviations) are shown in Table 24. Use of certificates and longer term deposits as financing has been statistically higher for the acquiring S&Ls. This relationship is consistent over all three years for which the data are available.

Table 24
RATIO OF PASSBOOK DEPOSITS TO TOTAL DEPOSITS
FOR MERGING S&LS
(In Percentage)

Year of Merger	Acquiring S&Ls	Acquired S&Ls	t Ratio
1972	55.33 (14.9)	57.63 (15.2)	−1.30*
1973	48.24 (15.4)	56.02 (21.7)	−3.28**
1974	47.15 (13.4)	52.06 (19.1)	−2.89**

*Significant at the 0.10 level.
**Significant at the .01 level.

As with the findings on the average size of mortgage (both conventional and overall), the average size of a deposit account of the acquiring S&Ls is significantly larger than that of the acquired S&Ls. This finding is consistent in each year of the analysis. Also, the proportion of depositors above the insured limit of the acquiring S&Ls is significantly higher. Given our finding concerning the average deposit account size, this relationship should be expected. Additionally, the proportion of depositors above the insured limit is larger for the acquiring associations in each year.

The ratio of net worth to total assets is not significantly different for acquiring and acquired S&Ls. For the mergers occuring from 1969 through 1972, the acquiring associations' mean ratio of net worth to total assets was slightly (and not significantly) higher than that of the acquired associations. The mergers in 1973 and 1974, however, were those in which the acquiring S&Ls had a mean net worth ratio less than that of the acquired S&Ls.

Cost Structure

Examination of selected measures of expenses reveals that there were significant differences in cost structure between acquiring and acquired S&Ls. The ratio of operating expenses to operating income was significantly higher for acquired S&Ls than for acquiring S&Ls, both over the aggregate period and in each year during the period. Nearly one-half of the total operating costs of acquiring and acquired S&Ls consisted of personnel compensation and directors' fees. Over the aggregate period, however, the ratio of personnel compensation and directors' fees to operating expenses is significantly higher for acquired S&Ls at a statistically significant level. Additionally, this relationship is consistent for each year during the period. The ratio of personnel compensation plus directors' fees to total deposits has the same relationship. Thus, it appears that in terms of compensation to all levels of management and nonmanagement personnel, acquired S&Ls were not as efficient in servicing and attracting deposits, nor were they as efficient in controlling other operating costs in lieu of higher personnel costs. This finding is consistent with the general hypotheses stated above.

The ratio of advertising expenses to operating expenses was significantly higher for acquiring S&Ls, as was the ratio of advertising expenses to total deposits. Therefore, in addition to requiring a relatively higher expenditure for advertising to obtain a given amount of deposits, acquiring S&Ls expended more in the advertising effort in relation to all other operating expenses. Both of these findings are consistent for each year of the study.

Acquired and acquiring S&Ls show contrasting relationships in their ratios of occupancy expenses to operating expenses and occupancy expenses to total assets. In terms of the aggregate period, acquiring S&Ls have a higher ratio of occupancy expenses to operating expenses at a level that is marginally significant, although the reverse is found in two of the six years analyzed. In contrast, their ratio of occupancy expenses to total assets is lower than that of the acquired S&Ls for the aggregate period and in five of the six individual years. Therefore, acquiring S&Ls show greater efficiency in maintaining and providing for the association's office(s). That these expenses in relation to all operating expenses are also greater for acquiring S&Ls is probably the result of the acquiring S&Ls' tendency to have more branches than acquired S&Ls.

The ratio of deposit interest (dividends) to operating income is significantly higher for acquired S&Ls for the aggregate period and for all years except 1969. Thus, for acquired associations, deposit costs comprise a larger burden on available funds. The tendency has been for acquiring S&Ls to pay a higher rate on savings deposits, however. This relationship is evident in the aggregate period analysis as well as for the last four years of the study (1971 through 1974).

We have noted that acquiring S&Ls hold a significantly higher level of higher-costing, nonpassbook deposits. Are the higher deposit costs of acquiring S&Ls attributable to a higher proportion of nonpassbook deposits, to a higher payment rate on deposits, or both? Using data available for associations merging in 1972, 1973, and 1974, Table 25 shows the means (and standard deviations) of interest/dividends paid on passbook and nonpassbook deposits as percentages of total passbook and nonpassbook deposits, respectively. There appears to be no consistent relationship in terms of nonpassbook deposit payments, but the passbook deposit dividends/interest was significantly higher for acquiring S&Ls in 1973 and 1974. Therefore, in bringing about higher deposit costs in relation to total deposits during those years, the acquiring S&Ls' tendency to have a higher ratio of nonpassbook deposits was magnified by the higher payment for passbook deposits.

The ratio of total operating expenses to operating income is significantly higher for the acquired S&Ls both over the aggregate and in each individual year. Thus, the expense coverage of the acquired S&Ls is found to be lower than that of the acquiring S&Ls.

Income Structure

All of the measures of income structure show significant differences between acquiring and acquired S&Ls in the aggregate period analysis, but the mortgage interest and income and operating income ratios vary somewhat over the individual years.

For acquired S&Ls the rate of income on mortgages is significantly higher in the aggregate period. This relationship holds for all years except 1974, when the acquiring S&Ls show a significantly higher mean rate of income on mortgages. Mortgage interest income as a proportion of gross income is higher for the acquiring S&Ls for the aggregate period at a marginally significant level, but the finding is consistent for only three of

Table 25
DIVIDENDS (INTEREST) PAID ON DEPOSITS
(In Percentage)

	Acquiring S&Ls	Acquired S&Ls	*t* Ratio
On Passbook Deposits			
1972	4.68 (0.04)	4.69 (0.8)	0.09
1973	5.10 (1.7)	4.71 (1.0)	1.60*
1974	5.04 (0.7)	4.92 (0.6)	1.46*
On Nonpassbook Deposits			
1972	5.05 (0.4)	4.99 (0.8)	0.54
1973	5.01 (0.8)	5.12 (0.9)	−0.43
1974	5.49 (0.9)	5.47 (0.9)	0.14

NOTE: Number at left = mean; in parentheses = standard deviation. All figures are percentages unless otherwise stated.

*Significant at the 0.10 level.

the six individual years. Thus, acquiring S&Ls appear to have had greater effectiveness in using assets to generate income, but the evidence for this finding is somewhat weak.

However, the ratios of income before tax to total assets and net income to total assets are significantly higher for acquiring S&Ls in both the aggregate and in each individual year. Therefore, although income generation from assets appears to be only slightly greater for acquiring S&Ls, the total expense incurred in supporting and servicing the assets is considerably less for acquiring S&Ls. This situation arises because, in relation to operating income, the two major expense areas—operating expenses and deposit interest (dividends)—both were found to be significantly higher for acquired S&Ls in the preceding analyses of the cost structure ratios. Another reflection of the higher cost structure is the ratio of net income to gross income, which is significantly higher for acquiring S&Ls in the aggregate and for each year. Net income to net worth, a measure of return to associations' ownership, is significantly higher for acquiring S&Ls in the aggregate. This general relationship is consistent for each year of the study.

All of the above relationships in asset structure, liability structure, cost structure, and income structure are useful in identifying major causes of the differences in return on assets and return on net worth (equity) between acquiring and acquired S&Ls. We will use the simple but informative model suggested by Cole.[5] The following expressions are relevant to this discussion:

(1) $\dfrac{\text{net income}}{\text{gross income}} \times \dfrac{\text{gross income}}{\text{assets}} = \dfrac{\text{net income}}{\text{assets}}$; and

     (profit margin)   (asset utilization) (return on assets)

(2) $\dfrac{\text{net income}}{\text{assets}} \times \dfrac{\text{assets}}{\text{equity}} = \dfrac{\text{net income}}{\text{equity}}$

  (return on assets) (equity multiplier) (return on equity)

First, one measure of profitability, the return on assets, can be analyzed as shown in Expression One.[6] The ratio of net income to gross income measures the degree of expense control or efficiency of operation. As noted before, mainly because of relatively higher personnel compensation expenses, acquired S&Ls had a lower mean net profit margin.[7] Much of the differential is most likely the result of economy-of-scale advantages which acquiring S&Ls enjoy over acquired S&Ls, some of which are based on acquiring S&Ls' larger average mortgages and deposits.

The ratio of gross income to assets indicates the gross yield on assets. An S&L may be able to produce a high return on assets despite a low profit margin if its asset utilization is sufficiently high. In this study the operating income to total assets ratio was only slightly higher for acquiring S&Ls for the aggregate period. Thus, we consider much of the difference in return on assets for acquiring and acquired S&Ls to be caused by the difference in operating expenses as opposed to the average return on invested assets.

Another measure of profitability is the ratio of net income to equity, or return on equity (net worth). As is noted in Expression Two, the return on equity is a function of the return on assets and the equity multiplier, which is the reciprocal of the ratio of net worth to assets. The equity multiplier is important, first, because it is a measure of risk. That is, as the use of financial leverage increases, the equity multiplier increases. Second, the return on equity is higher than the return on assets by a multiple which is equal to the equity multiplier. The equity multiplier for acquired associations is 14.6 and that of the acquiring associations 14.2. Thus, although there is some difference in equity multipliers, the major factor in effecting the difference in return on net worth between acquiring and acquired S&Ls (10.31 percent versus 6.36 percent) is the difference between the acquiring and acquired S&Ls in return on assets.

Comparisons of Acquisitions

Tables 26 through 27 contain means, standard deviations, and *t* ratios of the financial measures for those acquisitions made by state mutual, state stock, and federally chartered S&Ls, respectively. The purpose of

Table 26
ACQUISITIONS BY STATE MUTUAL ASSOCIATIONS, 1969 - 1974
Financial Ratio Comparison
(N=156)

	Acquiring Association	Acquired Association	*t* Ratio
Asset Structure			
Single family mortgages/ total mortgages	77.44 (14.4)	83.56 (15.7)	−4.64***
FHA and VA mortgages/ total mortgages	12.45 (14.7)	7.24 (15.8)	3.71***
Average conventional mortgage size (in $ thousands)	15.21 (6.6)	12.19 (5.1)	5.69***
Overall average mortgage size (in $ thousands)	14.26 (5.2)	12.08 (5.4)	4.71***
Total mortgages/ total assets	84.45 (5.9)	83.36 (6.8)	1.69**
Cash plus demand deposits/ total assets	2.11 (2.4)	3.75 (3.2)	−5.55***
Investments plus other liquid assets/ total assets	7.75 (3.9)	8.59 (5.4)	−1.97**
Fixed assets/ total assets	1.28 (0.8)	1.12 (1.2)	1.36*
Real estate owned and in judgment/ total assets	0.18 (0.3)	0.48 (1.1)	−3.39***
Nonconforming loans and contracts to facilitate sales of REO/ total mortgages	0.17 (0.4)	0.33 (0.8)	−2.73***
Liability Structure			
FHLBB advances/ total assets	2.86 (3.3)	2.02 (3.5)	2.51***
Borrowings other than from FHLBB/ total assets	0.61 (1.6)	0.71 (1.7)	−0.64
Total deposits/ total assets	86.32 (4.3)	87.93 (4.6)	−3.90***
Proportion of depositors with accounts above insured limit	1.27 (0.9)	1.06 (0.9)	2.55***
Average deposit account size (in $ thousands)	3.15 (0.8)	3.03 (1.3)	1.09
Net worth/total assets	6.81 (1.8)	7.08 (2.4)	−1.28

Continued

Table 26 (Continued)
(N=156)

	Acquiring Association	Acquired Association	*t* Ratio
Income Structure			
Interest income on mortgages/ total mortgages	6.26 (0.7)	6.38 (0.6)	−2.45***
Interest income on mortgages/ gross income	84.42 (5.0)	85.62 (5.0)	−2.50***
Operating income/ total assets	6.20 (0.5)	6.13 (0.4)	2.19***
Income before tax/ total assets	0.76 (0.4)	0.47 (0.7)	4.83***
Net income/gross income	9.61 (4.4)	5.86 (13.8)	3.40***
Net income/net worth	9.35 (4.7)	5.37 (14.1)	3.54***
Net income/total assets	0.60 (0.3)	0.38 (0.8)	3.59***
Cost Structure			
Personnel compensation plus directors' fees/ operating expenses	49.74 (6.0)	52.45 (8.8)	−3.39***
Personnel compensation plus directors' fees/ total deposits	0.66 (0.2)	0.74 (0.2)	−4.55***
Advertising expenses/ operating expenses	8.23 (3.9)	4.70 (4.1)	8.11***
Advertising expenses/ total deposits	0.11 (0.1)	0.07 (0.1)	5.65***
Occupancy expenses/ operating expenses	10.40 (4.7)	10.21 (5.2)	0.37
Occupancy expenses/ total assets	0.12 (0.1)	0.13 (0.1)	−1.51*
Deposit interest (dividends)/ operating income	66.37 (5.5)	67.73 (5.3)	−2.96***
Deposit interest (dividends)/ total deposits	4.79 (0.4)	4.76 (0.4)	0.73
Operating expenses/ operating income	18.24 (3.9)	20.40 (7.1)	−3.72***

NOTE: The number at the left represents the mean, and the number in parentheses represents the standard deviation. All numbers are percentages unless otherwise stated.
*Significant at the 0.10 level (one-tailed test).
**Significant at the 0.05 level (one-tailed test).
***Significant at the 0.01 level (one-tailed test).

Table 27
ACQUISITIONS BY STOCK ASSOCIATIONS, 1969 - 1974
Financial Ratio Comparison
(N=104)

	Acquiring Association	Acquired Association	*t* Ratio
Asset Structure			
Single family mortgages/ total mortgages	68.35 (14.4)	72.27 (16.5)	−2.03***
FHA and VA mortgages/ total mortgages	9.09 (16.4)	5.88 (11.5)	1.82**
Average conventional mortgage size (in $ thousands)	18.63 (5.6)	18.10 (6.5)	0.69
Overall average morgage size (in $ thousands)	18.35 (5.6)	18.47 (7.6)	−0.14
Total mortgages/ total assets	84.78 (9.7)	84.64 (6.0)	0.13
Cash plus demand deposits/ total assets	0.96 (1.6)	1.27 (1.7)	−1.45*
Investments plus other liquid assets/ total assets	7.44 (4.4)	7.82 (3.7)	−0.77
Fixed assets/ total assets	1.81 (2.2)	1.42 (1.0)	1.60*
Real estate owned and in judgment/ total assets	0.83 (1.6)	0.66 (1.1)	0.93
Nonconforming loans and contracts to facilitate sales of REO/ total mortgages	2.22 (.43)	1.32 (2.1)	1.99***
Liability Structure			
FHLBB advances/ total assets	9.57 (7.6)	6.95 (6.1)	3.49***
Borrowings other than from FHLBB/ total assets	0.91 (1.8)	0.37 (0.9)	2.86***
Total deposits/ total assets	80.49 (6.6)	81.75 (8.3)	--1.26**
Proportion of depositors with accounts above insured limit	1.46 (0.9)	1.17 (0.9)	2.92***
Average deposit account size (in $ thousands)	3.42 (0.9)	3.13 (0.8)	3.06***
Net worth/total assets	7.46 (4.1)	7.08 (2.2)	0.84

Continued

Table 27 (Continued)
(N=104)

	Acquiring Association	Acquired Association	*t* Ratio
Income Structure			
Interest income on mortgages/ total mortgages	6.87 (1.5)	6.78 (0.8)	0.61
Interest income on mortgages/ gross income	82.70 (3.6)	82.30 (4.2)	0.76
Operating income/ total assets	7.12 (2.3)	6.81 (0.5)	1.42*
Income before tax/ total assets	1.46 (3.3)	0.97 (0.7)	1.53*
Net income/gross income	11.33 (3.7)	10.69 (8.4)	0.70
Net income/net worth	11.68 (4.2)	9.46 (13.0)	1.66**
Net income/total assets	1.13 (2.8)	0.74 (0.6)	1.43*
Cost Structure			
Personnel compensation plus directors' fees/ operating expenses	42.36 (6.2)	43.81 (7.6)	−1.85**
Personnel compensation plus directors' fees/ total deposits	0.63 (0.2)	0.70 (0.2)	−2.51***
Advertising expenses/ operating expenses	11.33 (4.2)	9.30 (4.4)	4.01***
Advertising expenses/ total deposits	0.17 (0.1)	0.15 (0.1)	1.91**
Occupancy expenses/ operating expenses	12.83 (5.2)	11.01 (4.5)	2.87***
Occupancy expenses/ total assets	0.17 (0.1)	0.14 (0.1)	1.30
Deposit interest (dividends)/ operating income	58.53 (4.8)	59.32 (6.5)	−1.14
Deposit interest (dividends)/ total deposits	5.40 (2.5)	5.02 (0.8)	1.44*
Operating expenses/ operating income	16.67 (3.6)	18.83 (5.1)	−4.22***

NOTE: The number on the left represents the mean and the number in parentheses represents the standard deviation. All numbers are percentages unless otherwise stated.
*Significant at the 0.10 level (one-tailed test).
**Significant at the 0.05 level (one-tailed test).
***Significant at the 0.01 level (one-tailed test).

Table 28
ACQUISITIONS BY FEDERAL ASSOCIATIONS, 1969-1974
Financial Ratio Comparison
(N=250)

	Acquiring Association	Acquired Association	*t* Ratio
Asset Structure			
Single family mortgages/ total mortgages	78.24 (12.2)	80.45 (16.3)	−2.05***
FHA and VA mortgages/ total mortgages	13.86 (14.9)	5.42 (10.3)	8.62***
Average conventional mortgage size (in $ thousands)	17.12 (5.6)	13.53 (6.0)	8.47***
Overall average mortgage size (in $ thousands)	16.08 (5.2)	13.34 (5.9)	7.07***
Total mortgages/ total assets	83.71 (6.7)	83.57 (8.2)	0.22
Cash plus demand deposits/ total assets	1.16 (1.3)	2.99 (3.1)	−9.28***
Investments plus other liquid assets/ total assets	7.90 (3.3)	8.00 (4.7)	−0.27
Fixed assets/ total assets	1.55 (1.5)	1.25 (1.2)	2.58***
Real estate owned and in judgment/ total assets	0.22 (0.6)	0.35 (0.9)	−2.00***
Nonconforming loans and contract to facilitate sales of REO/ total mortgages	0.24 (0.6)	0.44 (1.8)	−1.75**
Liability Structure			
FHLBB advances/ total assets	5.70 (5.1)	3.99 (5.2)	4.49***
Borrowings other than from FHLBB/ total assets	0.44 (1.1)	0.55 (1.7)	−0.89
Total deposits/ total assets	83.01 (5.7)	85.63 (7.7)	−4.64***
Proportion of depositors with accounts above insured limit	1.51 (1.1)	1.19 (0.9)	4.77***
Average deposit account size (in $ thousands)	3.56 (1.2)	3.12 (1.0)	5.14***
Net worth/total assets	6.67 (2.3)	6.86 (3.4)	−0.86

Continued

Table 28 (Continued)
(N=250)

	Acquiring Association	Acquired Association	*t* Ratio
Income Structure			
Interest income on mortgages/ total mortgages	6.37 (1.0)	6.47 (0.8)	−1.40*
Interest income on mortgages/ gross income	83.07 (3.8)	83.62 (8.6)	−1.00
Operating income/ total assets	6.39 (1.1)	6.38 (0.7)	0.13
Income before tax/ total assets	0.84 (0.5)	0.54 (0.5)	6.55***
Net income/gross income	9.90 (4.2)	6.61 (7.2)	6.34***
Net income/net worth	10.33 (5.5)	5.68 (15.0)	4.65***
Net income/total assets	0.65 (0.4)	0.44 (0.5)	5.44***
Cost Structure			
Personnel compensation plus directors' fees/ operating expenses	48.44 (5.8)	51.66 (10.4)	−4.51***
Personnel compensation plus directors' fees/ total deposits	0.66 (0.2)	0.82 (0.3)	−6.88***
Advertising expenses/ operating expenses	10.10 (4.2)	6.27 (4.9)	10.13***
Advertising expenses/ total deposits	0.14 (0.1)	0.10 (0.1)	4.78***
Occupancy expenses/ operating expenses	11.49 (4.9)	11.28 (7.7)	0.37
Occupancy expenses/ total assets	0.14 (0.1)	0.16 (0.1)	−2.00***
Deposit interest (dividends)/ operating income	64.24 (5.7)	65.25 (7.3)	−1.91**
Deposit interest (dividends)/ total deposits	4.95 (1.0)	4.89 (0.5)	0.92
Operating expenses/ operating income	17.66 (3.6)	21.08 (8.0)	−6.51***

NOTE: The number on the left represents the mean and the number in parentheses represents the standard deviation. All numbers are percentages unless otherwise stated.
*Significant at the 0.10 level (one-tailed test).
**Significant at the 0.05 level (one-tailed test).
***Significant at the 0.01 level (one-tailed test).

this analysis is to determine if the acquiring and acquired S&Ls showed different financial relationships when the acquiring S&Ls were of different types.

The tables show that the acquiring and acquired S&Ls are most similar when the acquirer is a stock S&L. First, there are no significant differences between the acquiring and acquired S&Ls in average conventional and overall average mortgage sizes in the state stock mergers. On the other hand, in the state mutual and federal mergers, the acquiring S&Ls have significantly higher average mortgage loan sizes than do the acquired S&Ls. Second, the ratio of the real estate owned (REO) and in judgment to total mortgages and the ratio of nonconforming loans and contracts to facilitate sales of REO to total mortgages are *higher* for the acquiring S&Ls than for the acquired S&Ls in the state stock mergers. These two measures of the degree of loan default are significantly lower for the acquiring S&Ls in the federal and state mutual mergers.

Third, non-FHLBB borrowing is significantly higher for the acquiring S&Ls in the state stock mergers, whereas the ratios of non-FHLBB borrowing in acquiring versus acquired S&Ls in the federal and state mutual mergers show no significant differences.

Fourth, no significant difference exists in the net profit margins (net income to gross income) between the acquiring and acquired S&Ls in the state stock mergers, whereas in the federal and state mutual mergers the net profit margins are significantly higher for the acquiring S&Ls.

The reason for these differences can be traced to the general characteristics of stock S&Ls compared to mutual S&Ls. Hester[8] and others have found that stock associations are more aggressive and undertake more investment risks than mutual S&Ls. Thus, large stock S&Ls have more foreclosures and own more real estate relative to small stock S&Ls than is the case for state mutual and federal S&Ls. Hester further reported that stock S&Ls have larger average mortgage loan sizes than mutuals and thus their asset portfolios are less diversified. In line with Hester's finding, this study found that the average mortgage loan was higher for the acquiring and acquired S&Ls in the stock mergers than for those in the federal and state mutual mergers. The significantly higher non-FHLBB borrowing for the acquiring S&Ls in the stock mergers is also related to the aggressiveness of stock S&Ls.

Finally, Hester reported that stock S&Ls typically have lower net profit margins than mutual S&Ls. This relationship is also found in our results. In addition, the net profit margin advantage of large (acquiring) stock S&Ls over small (acquired) stock S&Ls is not significant. The economies of scale which were anticipated to be advantageous to acquiring stock S&Ls do not occur.

Although we did find differences between the results of stock mergers and of mutual (federal and state mutual) mergers, overall the differences between the acquiring and acquired S&Ls in each type of merger are quite similar. Furthermore for each type of merger, the two general measures of performance—net income to total assets and net income to net worth—are higher for the acquiring than for the acquired S&L.

Implications

The evidence indicates that overall, acquiring S&Ls tended to absorb institutions significantly different from themselves in terms of the financial characteristics examined. As hypothesized, the acquired S&Ls showed a poorer performance than the acquiring S&Ls in terms of profit before taxes to total assets, net income to total assets, and net income to net worth. There is evidence that the acquiring S&Ls were more efficient than the acquired S&Ls, since the acquiring S&Ls had significantly lower ratios of operating expenses to operating income and of personnel compensation expenses to total deposits than did the acquired S&Ls.

Of the three types of S&Ls, however, acquiring stock S&Ls tended to perform more similarly to the associations they acquired (all of which were stock S&Ls) than did acquiring federal or state mutual S&Ls. The more aggressive nature of stock S&Ls probably caused this result. Finally, the evidence shows that the acquisitions of the acquiring S&Ls provided them with liquidity and asset diversification, along with the geographical diversification and growth which explicitly follow from mergers of S&Ls.

NOTES

1. For example, see Dennis C. Mueller, "A Theory of Conglomerate Mergers," *Quarterly Journal of Economics,* Nov. 1967.

2. Eugene F. Brigham and R. Richardson Pettit, "Effects of Structure on Performance of the Savings and Loan Industry," in *Study of the Savings and Loan Industry,* ed. by Irwin Friend (Washington, D.C.: Government Printing Office, 1969), p. 1069.

3. *Ibid.,* p. 1062.

4. Specifically, the breakdown is (1) savings accounts earning in excess of the regular rate paid on passbook accounts, and (2) savings accounts earning at or below the regular rate paid on passbook savings.

5. D.W. Cole, "Measuring Savings and Loan Profitability," *Federal Home Loan Bank Board Journal,* Oct. 1971.

6. See Cole, "Measuring Savings and Loan Profitability" for a derivation and extensive discussion of these relationships.

7. Note that operating income is about 99 percent of gross income for the associations in the study.

8. Donald D. Hester, *Stock and Mutual Associations in the Savings and Loan Industry* (Washington, D.C.: Federal Home Loan Bank Board, 1968).

IV

THE PERFORMANCE OF
MERGING SAVINGS AND LOAN ASSOCIATIONS

Chapters 2 and 3 examined the changes in ownership and charter structure of the savings and loan industry as a result of merger and compared the financial characteristics of acquiring and acquired associations.

An important extension of those analyses to which this chapter is devoted, is to compare the financial characteristics and performance of acquiring S&Ls to a matched group of nonmerging S&Ls. Specifically, eighty-three merged S&Ls will be compared with eighty-three non-merging S&Ls for the year prior to, and for both two and three years following the year of merger, for mergers occuring in 1969, 1970, and 1971.

First, this chapter will detail the criteria used in selecting the nonmerging associations for comparison and will introduce the hypotheses and tests. Then it will compare acquired, acquiring, and nonmerging associations with respect to balance sheet and operating characteristics in the year prior to the year of merger. Finally, it will compare the financial performances of the nonmerging and acquiring S&Ls for two and three years after the merger.

Background

The criteria employed to select the nonmerging S&Ls for the comparison sample were:
1. Location of the home office of each nonmerging S&L in the same SMSA or county as the home office of its corresponding acquiring S&L
2. The same general asset size as the corresponding acquiring S&L in the year prior to the year of merger
3. Not having been merged with five years prior to or three years after the year of merger of its corresponding acquiring S&L
4. Being of the same type (state stock, state mutual, or federal) as its corresponding acquiring S&L.

67

A total of 257 regular (nonsupervisory) mergers occurred between FSLIC-insured associations in the January 1969 through December 1971 period. These 257 mergers involved acquisitions by 174 S&Ls because some associations made more than one acquisition during the period. Given the controls placed on the nonmerging sample, we were able to select eighty-three S&Ls for which two- and three-year postmerger comparisons could be made.

Tests and hypotheses

As noted earlier, a number of authors maintain that the possibility of operating economies (and thus higher profitability) is the only justification for a merger when the objective of the firm is to maximize the owners' wealth. The magnitude of operating economies provided by merger for S&Ls will be examined by comparing selected financial performance measures of the acquiring S&Ls with the matched nonmerging S&Ls for the year before the merger, and for two and three years after the year of merger. Changes in the relation of these measures between the acquiring and nonmerging S&Ls will be examined and related to the effect of merger on the acquiring S&L. The relationships observed can be expressed mathematically as:

$$(1) \qquad \Delta P_{ij} = (p_{ij}^{a} - p_{ib}^{a}) - (p_{ij}^{n} - p_{ib}^{n}) \qquad j = 2,3$$

where p_{ib}^{a} represents the value of performance measure i for the acquiring S&L in the year previous to the year of merger; p_{ij}^{a} represents the value of performance measure i for the acquiring S&L in the second [$j = 2$] or third [$j = 3$] year after the year of merger; and p_{ib}^{n} and p_{ij}^{n} are the corresponding measures for the matched nonmerging S&L. Performance is measured by balance sheet and income statement variables relating to lending and investment characteristics, financial structure, and revenues and expenses. Correlated "t" tests will be performed on the 83 pairs of S&Ls to determine if any significant differences exist in performance changes over the two- and three-year periods following merger.[1]

Our general hypothesis in the performance tests is that no differences exist between nonmerging S&Ls and acquiring S&Ls in changes in performance (that is, $\Delta P_{ij} = 0$). This hypothesis rests with the assumption that the choice of growth through merger and through internal growth (branching, etc.) is a random phenomenon among S&Ls, so that over time the changes in performance resulting from these two paths of growth are equal.

Thus far, no studies have been conducted to examine the differences that exist between S&Ls which have made acquisitions and comparable S&Ls which have not. The magnitude of difference (D_i) in financial measure i between acquiring, acquired, and nonmerging S&Ls can be expressed as:

$$D_i(1) = p_{ib}^n - p_{ib}^a \tag{2}$$

$$D_i(2) = p_{ib}^n - p_{ib}^s \tag{3}$$

$$D_i(3) = p_{ib}^a - p_{ib}^s \tag{4}$$

where p_{ib}^s represents the value of performance measure i of the acquired S&L in the year preceding the merger and all other terms are as previously defined. The null hypothesis tested in expresions (2), (3), and (4) is that $D_i(1) = 0$; that is, that there is no difference in financial characteristics between acquiring and nonmerging S&Ls. This results from the above assumption that internal and external growth are randomly distributed among S&Ls. Differences between the acquired S&Ls and the other two groups (acquiring and nonmerging) have been hypothesized in Chapter 3.

Premerger Comparisons

Table 29 contains the means, standard deviations, and t ratios of selected financial measures for the nonmerging (NON), acquiring (ACG), and acquired (AQD) savings and loans. The financial ratios refer to the year prior to merger of the S&Ls.

Asset and liability structure

The AQG group has significantly lower ratios of insured mortgages to total mortgages, cash plus demand deposits to total assets, and real estate owned and in judgment to total assets than does the NON group. The AQG group also has significantly higher ratios of single family mortgages to total mortgages, average mortgage size, and proportion of assets held in mortgages than the NON group.

With respect to the AQG-AQD group comparisons, the study found that the AQG group has significantly lower cash-plus-demand deposits to total assets, and significantly higher insured mortgages to total mortgages, average mortgage size, total mortgages to total assets, fixed assets to total assets, and nonconforming loans to total mortgages than the AQG group.

These same relationships are found in comparing the NON group and the AQD group, with the following exceptions: the NON group has significantly lower single-family mortgages and higher nonconforming loans than the AQD group, whereas no statistical differences were found in the AQG-AQD comparison in these measures, and there is no significant difference between the NON group and the AQD group in the ratios of their fixed assets to total assets, although there is a significant difference when the AQG and AQD groups are compared.

In contrast to the findings for asset structure, no differences are found between the AQD and NON groups in the liability structure measures used here. In addition, both the AQD and NON groups have significantly

Table 29
FINANCIAL COMPARISONS
(N=83)

	(1) Nonmerging S&Ls	(2) Acquiring S&Ls	(3) Acquired S&Ls	t Ratio D(1) 1-2	t Ratio D(2) 1-3	t Ratio D(3) 1-4
Asset Structure						
Single family mortgages/ total mortgages	72.37 (14.9)	76.96 (14.1)	78.39 (19.4)	-2.83***	-2.69***	-0.66
FHA and VA mortgages/ total mortgages	13.02 (17.0)	8.34 (13.1)	3.34 (9.0)	2.64***	5.10***	3.98***
Average conventional mortgage size (in $ thousands)	14.05 (4.5)	14.57 (5.0)	12.50 (5.0)	-0.95	2.80***	4.35***
Overall average mortgage size (in $ thousands)	13.80 (4.0)	14.29 (4.6)	12.34 (4.9)	-1.21	2.68***	4.35***
Total mortgages/ total assets	86.06 (3.9)	86.72 (2.8)	84.34 (10.2)	-1.47*	1.41*	2.21**
Cash plus demand deposits/ total assets	2.29 (2.3)	1.95 (2.0)	3.50 (2.9)	1.62*	-3.59***	-4.59***
Investments plus other liquid assets/ total assets	6.63 (2.8)	6.45 (2.2)	6.00 (3.9)	0.51	1.24	1.05
Fixed assets/ total assets	1.44 (1.0)	1.52 (0.9)	1.28 (1.1)	-0.48	0.93	1.37*
Real estate owned and in judgment/ total assets	0.49 (1.3)	0.26 (0.4)	0.37 (0.8)	1.70**	0.73	-1.10
Nonconforming loans and contracts to facilitate sales of REO/ total mortgages	0.67 (1.9)	0.44 (1.1)	0.39 (0.8)	1.14	1.51*	0.48

Continued

Table 29 (Continued)
(N=83)

	(1) Nonmerging S&Ls	(2) Acquiring S&Ls	(3) Acquired S&Ls	t Ratio D(1) 1-1	t Ratio D(2) 1-3	t Ratio D(3) 2-3
Liability Structure						
FHLBB advances/ total assets	5.96 (6.4)	5.42 (5.1)	4.23 (5.4)	0.86	2.45***	1.79**
Borrowings other than from FHLBB/ total assets	0.17 (0.5)	0.26 (1.1)	0.26 (0.67)	-0.85	-1.10	0.02
Total deposits/ total assets	83.63 (6.4)	83.97 (5.7)	83.94 (12.5)	-0.53	-0.21	0.05
Proportion of depositors with accounts above insured limit	0.82 (0.7)	0.80 (0.7)	0.76 (0.7)	0.24	0.83	0.44
Average deposit account size (in $ thousands)	2.89 (0.7)	2.86 (0.7)	2.58 (0.8)	0.31	2.85***	2.65***
Net worth/total assets	7.05 (1.9)	7.31 (1.6)	7.37 (3.4)	-1.00	-0.65	-0.12
Income Structure						
Interest income on mortgages/ total mortgages	5.99 (1.5)	5.97 (0.4)	6.06 (0.9)	0.59	-0.67	-1.04
Interest income on mortgages/ gross income	85.41 (3.8)	85.30 (3.5)	84.47 (22.4)	0.24	0.71	0.68
Operating income/ total assets	5.98 (0.4)	6.04 (0.4)	6.01 (0.9)	-1.60*	-0.37	0.18
Income before tax/ total assets	0.62 (0.4)	0.65 (0.3)	0.51 (0.4)	-0.67	1.27	2.53***
Net income/gross income	8.65 (5.7)	8.96 (3.7)	7.05 (6.6)	-0.47	1.65*	2.47***
Net income/net worth	7.77 (5.9)	7.71 (3.6)	6.87 (8.2)	0.09	0.87	0.95
Net income/total assets	0.52 (0.3)	0.54 (0.2)	0.44 (0.4)	-0.59	1.27	2.15**

Continued

Table 29 (Continued)
N = 83

	(1) Nonmerging S&Ls	(2) Acquiring S&Ls	(3) Acquired S&Ls	t Ratio		
				D(1) 1-1	D(2) 1-3	D(3) 2-3
Cost Structure						
Personnel compensation plus directors' fees/ operating expenses	47.42 (6.7)	48.29 (6.6)	49.35 (10.4)	−1.02	−1.44*	−0.78
Personnel compensation plus directors' fees/ total deposits	0.65 (0.2)	0.68 (0.2)	0.78 (0.3)	−1.73**	−3.30***	−2.49***
Advertising expenses/ operating expenses	8.72 (4.2)	9.32 (4.6)	5.78 (4.2)	−1.27	4.92***	5.24***
Advertising expenses/ total deposits	0.12 (0.1)	0.13 (0.1)	0.09 (0.1)	−0.96	2.71***	3.39***
Occupancy expenses/ operating expenses	11.81 (5.7)	12.02 (6.3)	12.00 (6.9)	−0.25	−0.18	−0.06
Occupancy expenses/ total assets	0.14 (0.1)	0.14 (0.1)	0.16 (0.1)	−0.42	−1.36*	−1.13
Deposit interest (dividends)/ operating income	64.79 (6.0)	64.98 (5.3)	64.57 (9.3)	−0.29	0.19	0.56
Deposit interest (dividends)/ total deposits	4.64 (0.4)	4.66 (0.3)	4.68 (1.1)	−0.79	−0.38	−0.11
Operating expenses/ operating income	19.21 (4.1)	19.62 (3.6)	21.69 (8.2)	−0.85	−2.63***	−2.20**

NOTE: The number on the left represents the mean and the number in parentheses represents the standard deviation. All numbers are percentages unless otherwise stated.
*Significant at the 0.10 level.
**Significant at the 0.05 level.
***Significant at the 0.01 level.

higher ratios of FHLB advances to total assets and larger mean deposit accounts than do the AQD group.

Income structure

The AQG group has a significantly higher ratio of operating income to total assets than the NON group. The other measures of income structure show no statistically significant differences, however. In the AQG - AQD comparisons, the AQG group has significantly higher ratios of income before tax to total assets, net income after tax to total assets, and net income to gross income than does the AQD group. These same general relationships are found in the NON - AQD comparisons, but the differences between the NON and AQD groups in net income before tax and after tax to total assets are not statistically significant.

Cost structure

The ratio of personnel compensation to total deposits for the AQG group is significantly higher than that of the NON group. Otherwise, there are no significant differences in cost structure between the AQG and NON groups. In contrast, the AQG group has a higher ratio of advertising expenses to operating expenses and of advertising expenses to total deposits than does the AQD group. Also, the AQG group has significantly lower ratios of personnel compensation to total deposits and of operating expenses to operating income than the AQD group. These same relationships are found in the NON - AQD comparisons, with the following exceptions: the ratios of occupancy expenses to total assets and of personnel compensation to operating expenses of the NON group are significantly lower than those of the AQG group, whereas no significant differences in these ratios are found in the AQG-AQD comparisons.

Overall comparisons of acquiring and nonmerging S&Ls

On balance, the business risks of the acquiring and nonmerging S&Ls are quite similar, although there are points of significant difference between the two groups in asset distribution. Nonmerging S&Ls hold a higher proportion of their assets in multifamily mortgages and in insured mortgages, both of which typically have higher default risk than single-family and conventional mortgages, respectively. The higher default risk in the mortgage portfolios of the nonmerging S&Ls is reflected in the significantly higher proportion of real estate owned and in judgment to total morgages which they show in comparison to acquiring S&Ls. It it also found, however, that nonmerging S&Ls have a significantly higher proportion of assets invested in cash and demand deposits, which implies that the higher default risk in their portfolios is offset somewhat by these holdings.

On the cost side, acquiring S&Ls pay more than nonmerging S&Ls for personnel expenses per dollar of deposits. The most significant comparisons, however, are those involving general measures of performance. Acquiring S&Ls produce more operating income per dollar of assets than do nonmerging S&Ls, but there are no significant differences between the two groups' ratios of income before tax to total assets, net income to total assets, net income to gross income, or net income to net worth. Thus, the major financial performance measures of the two groups are quite similar in the year prior to the year of merger of the acquiring associations.

Multivariate comparisons for the premerger period

It is possible to determine which combination of financial measures best distinguishes between the acquiring, nonmerging, and acquired S&Ls by using multivariate discriminant analysis (MDA). In addition to the financial measures shown in Table 29, the log of total assets was included as a discriminant variable to consider the size of attribute when the MDA model was run. Also, the log of the mean deposit account size was substituted for the absolute mean deposit account size to decrease the effect of scale differences between the financial measures.

The discriminant analysis algorithm was run using the above-mentioned variables, a stepwise variable selection process, and the Mahalonobis Distance between the groups as the criterion for selecting variables to be included in the discriminant function.[2] The results of the MDA exercise for the three groups are show in Table 30.

As expected, the results show that acquiring and nonmerging S&Ls are more similar to each other than either is to acquired S&Ls. This conclusion is implied by the predicted groupings in Table 30A. In addition, the acquired S&Ls are more similar to nonmerging S&Ls than to acquiring S&Ls.[3]

The eigenvalues and their associated canonical correlations shown in Table 30B denote the relative discriminating ability of the two functions shown in Table 30C. Although Function 1 has about 91 percent of the discriminating power, Function 2 is stilll marginally significant. The absolute size of the standardized discriminant function coefficients are estimates of the relative importance of each variable in separating the three groups.[4] Interest income on mortgages to total morgages, or the average mortgage interest rate, is the best predictor variable. As expected, the log of total assets is also an important discriminator. This results from the size differentials between the acquired S&Ls and both the nonmerging and acquiring S&Ls. The third most important discriminator is the ratio of operating income to total assets.

Since the primary interest of this paper is the financial characteristics of the acquiring S&Ls compared to those of the matched nonmerging S&Ls, a discriminant analysis was conducted on only those two groups,

Table 30

RESULTS OF THE THREE-GROUP DISCRIMINANT ANALYSIS

A.

Actual Group Membership		Predicted Group Membership		
Category	Number	Acquired S&Ls	Acquiring S&Ls	Nonmerging S&Ls
Acquired S&Ls	83 100.0%	63 75.9%	9 10.8%	11 13.3%
Acquiring S&Ls	83 100.0%	12 14.5%	42 50.6%	29 34.9%
Nonmerging S&Ls	83 100.0%	14 16.9%	16 19.3%	53 63.9%

Overall Correct Classifications: 63.45%

B.

Discriminant Function	Eigenvalue	Relative Percentage	Wilks's Lambda	Chi-Square	DF	Significance
1	0.6760	90.75	0.5582	141.093	18	0.000
2	0.0689	9.25	0.9355	16.130	8	0.041

C.

Variable	Standardized Discriminant Function Coefficients	
	Function 1	Function 2
Log assets	−0.33616	−0.13630
Log mean deposit account size	−0.00180	0.13782
Single family mortgages/total mortgages	0.00755	−0.16448
FHA and VA mortgages/total mortgages	−0.02552	0.20970
Net worth/total asssets	−0.05518	−0.08354
Interest income on mortgages/total mortgages	−0.56310	0.28394
Operating income/total assets	0.18253	−0.27419
Advertising expenses/operating expenses	−0.07390	−0.02289
Deposit interest/total deposits	0.05838	−0.01477

using the same variables except log of total assets. The purpose of this test is to determine (1) the set of financial measures which best distinguishes between acquiring and comparable nonmerging S&Ls, and (2) how well the set of financial measures can distinguish between the two groups of S&Ls. Before conducting these analyses, 20 pairs of acquiring and nonmerging S&Ls (40 total) were randomly selected as a holdout sample. The 63 pairs of acquiring and nonmerging S&Ls were used as the original test sample, and the results of this discriminant analysis are shown in Table 31.

It is seen that, although the predicted groupings on the original test sample in Table 31A are 70.3 percent correct, the classification on the holdout sample is only 50 percent correct. This latter percentage is more meaningful theoretically since it shows that the financial measures cannot be used in groups to distinguish between the two groups of S&Ls to any significant extent.[5] It addition, the discriminant function described in 31B is only marginally significant. Interpretation of the relative influence of the measures as discriminators is difficult because of the large number of measures in the final discriminant function and the intercorrelations between many of the variables.

The discriminant exercises summarized in this section lead to the conclusion that there are discernible differences between acquired S&Ls and both acquiring and nonmerging S&Ls with respect to overall financial characteristics. With respect to S&Ls which made acquisitions and comparable S&Ls which did not make acquisitions, however, it is difficult to discriminate between these groups using the financial measures considered in this study.

Postmerger Comparisons
Consistent differences

Five financial characteristics which were significantly different between merging and nonmerging S&Ls in the year prior to merger were also found to be significantly different in the third year after merger. Column 6 in Table 32 shows that the proportion of mortgages on single-family housing remains significantly higher for acquiring S&Ls.

Additionally, the proportion of total mortgages held in FHA and VA insured mortgages and the proportion of total assets held in cash and demand deposits remain significantly higher for the nonmerging S&Ls. Another area of consistent difference between the groups is the amount of gross operating income to total assets. This measure of performance remains significantly higher for the acquiring S&Ls.

The ratio of personnel compensation to total deposits is also higher for the acquiring S&Ls in both the premerger and postmerger periods. These findings suggest that several characteristic differences exist between acquiring and nonmerging S&Ls and that these differences remain relatively stable over time.

Table 31

RESULTS OF THE TWO-GROUP DISCRIMINANT ANALYSIS OF
ACQUIRING AND NONMERGING
SAVINGS AND LOAN ASSOCIATIONS

A.

Actual Group Membership		Predicted Group Membership			
		Acquiring S&Ls		Nonmerging S&Ls	
Category	Number	Number	%	Number	%
Original: Acquiring S&Ls	63	22	34.9	41	(65.1)
Nonmerging S&Ls	63	48	76.2	15	(23.8)
Holdout: Acquiring S&Ls	20	11	55.0	9	(45.0)
Nonmerging S&Ls	20	11	55.0	9	(45.0)

Correct classifications, original sample = 70.6%
Correct classifications, holdout group = 50.0%

B.

Eigenvalue	Canonical Correlation	Wilks's Lambda	Chi-Square	DF	Significance
0.24371	0.443	.8040	25.300	16	0.065

C.

Variable	Standardized Discriminant Function Coefficients
Log mean deposit account size	−0.01476
Single family mortgages/total mortgages	−0.06451
FHA and VA mortgages/total mortgages	0.04175
Nonconforming loans, etc.,/total mortgages	−0.05065
FHLBB advances/total assets	−0.25447
Borrowings/total assets	−0.04842
Total deposits/total assets	−0.24456
Net worth/total assets	−0.03031
Interest income on mortgages/total mortgages	0.12205
Net income/total assets	0.32588
Net income/gross income	−0.46354
Interest income on mortgages/gross income	−0.01787
Personnel compensation/operating expenses	−0.08623
Operating expenses/operating income	−0.21830
Deposit interest/total deposits	−0.24296
Personnel compensation to total deposits	0.08661

Table 32

FINANCIAL COMPARISONS OF NONMERGING AND ACQUIRING SAVINGS AND LOAN ASSOCIATIONS TWO AND THREE YEARS AFTER MERGER

Measure	(1) Nonmerging S&Ls i+2	(2) Acquiring S&Ls i+2	(3) Nonmerging S&Ls i+3	(4) Acquiring S&Ls i+3	(5) t Ratio 1–2	(6) t Ratio 3–4	(7) ΔP_{12}	(8) ΔP_{13}
Asset Structure								
Single family mortgages/ total mortgages	76.00 (17.5)	76.90 (12.7)	74.43 (17.8)	77.98 (16.6)	−0.47	−1.69**	2.53***	0.58
FHA and VA mortgages/ total mortgages	18.51 (24.7)	10.08 (14.6)	16.95 (21.9)	10.81 (18.2)	3.29***	2.57***	2.63***	1.21
Average conventional mortgage size (in $ thousands)	20.00 (7.0)	19.93 (6.2)	19.36 (9.1)	20.05 (8.5)	0.08	−0.70	−0.52	−0.69
Overall average mortgage size (in $ thousands)	19.83 (7.4)	19.85 (6.1)	19.10 (9.2)	19.53 (8.4)	−0.03	−0.42	−0.23	−0.28
Total mortgages/ total assets	81.98 (9.5)	83.94 (4.9)	81.29 (8.9)	82.22 (6.9)	−2.20**	−1.21	−1.38*	0.13
Cash plus demand deposits/ total assets	1.57 (1.6)	1.20 (1.2)	1.66 (2.0)	0.95 (1.0)	1.70**	3.02***	0.05	1.17
Investments plus other liquid assets/ total assets	8.32 (3.1)	7.81 (2.4)	7.64 (3.5)	7.08 (2.2)	1.54*	1.31*	1.08	0.97
Fixed assets/ total assets	1.35 (0.9)	1.40 (0.8)	1.35 (0.9)	1.43 (0.7)	−0.33	−0.66	0.26	−0.03
Real estate owned and in judgment/ total assets	0.18 (0.5)	0.20 (0.6)	0.19 (0.5)	0.30 (0.6)	−0.32	−1.35*	−1.42*	−2.18**
Nonconforming loans and contracts to facilitate sales of REO/ total mortgages	0.23 (0.6)	0.08 (0.3)	0.24 (0.6)	0.11 (0.3)	2.42***	2.11**	0.96	0.84

Liability Structure								
FHLBB advances/ total assets	4.39(4.0)	5.22(4.8)	5.83(4.8)	6.35(5.5)	-1.44*	-0.83	-2.46***	-1.92**
Borrowings other than from FHLBB/ total assets	0.60(1.1)	0.94(1.6)	0.73(1.4)	0.75(1.4)	-1.71**	-0.11	-1.23	0.33
Total deposits/ total assets	84.46(4.7)	83.01(5.6)	82.02(10.5)	82.44(-6.3)	2.58***	-0.32	3.01***	-0.06
Proportion of depositors with accounts above insured limit	1.55(0.7)	1.63(0.8)	1.02(1.0)	1.01(1.0)	-0.83	0.21	-0.92	-0.08
Average deposit account size (in $ thousands)	3.59(0.8)	3.49(0.8)	3.76(0.8)	3.66(0.8)	1.19	0.94	1.22	-0.27
Net worth/total assets	6.57(2.0)	6.53(1.5)	6.47(2.1)	6.54(1.7)	0.14	-0.23	1.88**	0.94
Income Structure								
Interest income on mortgages/ total mortgages	6.69(0.8)	6.79(1.1)	6.89(1.1)	7.05(0.8)	-1.27	-1.01	-1.70**	-1.42*
Interest income on mortgages/ gross income	83.00(5.1)	83.46(4.2)	81.64(11.5)	83.42(4.0)	-0.78	-1.44*	-1.11	-1.56*
Operating income/ total assets	6.52(0.6)	6.57(0.5)	6.74(0.9)	6.93(0.5)	-0.90	-1.94**	0.32	-1.27
Income before tax/ total assets	0.82(0.4)	0.81(0.4)	0.76(0.5)	0.74(0.5)	0.10	0.23	0.47	0.69
Net income/gross income	9.02(3.7)	8.93(3.6)	7.48(4.4)	7.35(4.6)	0.16	0.22	0.58	0.64
Net income/	9.95(5.9)	9.37(4.3)	7.89(5.4)	7.81(5.4)	0.78	0.11	0.62	0.02
Net income/total assets	0.67(0.5)	0.61(0.5)	0.58(0.4)	0.57(0.4)	0.90	0.19	1.23	0.61

Continued

Table 32 (Continued)

Measure	(1) Nonmerging S&Ls i+2	(2) Acquiring S&Ls i+2	(3) Nonmerging S&Ls i+3	(4) Acquiring S&Ls i+3	t Ratio (5) 1—2	(6) 3—4	(7) ΔP_{i2}	(8) ΔP_{i3}
Cost Structure								
Personnel compensation plus directors' fees/ operating expenses	47.32(6.7)	50.70(6.1)	47.45(8.8)	51.37(6.4)	-3.65***	-3.57***	-2.82***	-2.75***
Personnel compensation plus directors' fees/ total deposits	0.77(0.4)	0.92(0.3)	0.76(0.2)	0.86(0.2)	-2.53***	-1.52*	-2.17**	0.18
Advertising expenses/ operating expenses	9.12(4.6)	9.26(4.0)	9.13(5.2)	10.58(5.1)	-0.26	-2.14**	0.78	-1.10
Advertising expenses/ total deposits	0.12(0.1)	0.13(0.1)	0.11(0.1)	0.12(0.1)	-1.15	-0.56	-0.06	-0.01
Occupancy expenses/ operating expenses	10.39(4.8)	9.78(3.3)	10.36(4.3)	10.58(3.7)	0.94	-0.35	0.90	0.00
Occupancy expenses/ total assets	0.12(0.1)	0.11(0.0)	0.11(0.1)	0.12(0.1)	0.42	-0.70	-0.19	0.20
Deposit interest (dividends)/ operating income	5.04(0.2)	5.08(0.4)	5.30(0.7)	5.37(0.5)	-0.83	-0.78	-0.16	-0.42
Deposit interest (dividends)/ total deposits	65.39(5.7)	64.23(5.1)	64.23(8.9)	64.20(5.6)	1.95**	0.11	2.10**	0.28
Operating expenses/ operating income	17.14(3.6)	17.64(3.9)	16.65(3.9)	16.99(3.3)	-1.01	-0.77	-0.20	0.13

NOTE: i represents the year in which the acquiring S&L merged.
*Significant at the 0.10 level.
**Significant at the 0.05 level.
***Significant at the 0.01 level.

Changes in performance

As column 9 in Table 32 shows, there were several significant differences between the acquiring and nonmerging S&Ls in changed performance during the three-year, postmerger period. First, the REO/total mortages ratio decreased for the nonmerging S&Ls during the three-year, postmerger period, whereas this ratio increased for the acquiring S&Ls. This finding is interesting because it contrasts with the other measure of loan default, the ratio of nonconforming loans to total mortgages. Although acquiring S&Ls had a significantly higher mean ratio of REO to total mortgages than the nonmerging S&Ls in the third year after merger, they had a significantly lower mean ratio of nonconforming loans to total mortgages.

Second, the increase in the ratio of FHLB advances to total assets is significantly greater for the acquiring S&Ls than for the nonmerging S&Ls during the three-year postmerger period, although in the premerger year comparisons the nonmerging associations were found to use FHLB advances to a significantly higher degree than acquiring S&Ls. The change after the merger period results in there being no significant difference between the acquiring and nonmerging S&Ls in the use of advances for the three-year postmerger period overall.

Third, acquiring S&Ls showed significantly higher increases in average interest rate paid on mortgages and the proportion of gross income provided by mortgage interest income than did nomerging S&Ls over the three-year, postmerger period. The average mortgage interest rate of the acquiring S&Ls is lower than that of the nonmerging S&Ls in the premerger year but higher than that of the nonmerging S&Ls in the third year after the year of merger. The differences in both instances are statistically insignificant, however. The relative change in the proportion of gross income provided by mortgage interest income from the one-year, premerger period to the three-year, postmerger period results in a significantly higher ratio for acquiring S&Ls in this measure for the four years overall. This finding appears to result from reinforcing relationships—i.e., that acquiring S&Ls have a significantly lower mean proportion of cash and investments to total assets, and a higher mean return rate on mortgages than nonmerging S&Ls in the third year after the year of merger.

Fourth, during the three-year postmerger period there was a significantly larger increase in the ratio of personnel compensation to operating expenses for the acquiring S&Ls than for the nonmerging S&Ls. The relative change in the proportion of operating expenses composed of personnel compensation results in a significantly higher ratio for the acquiring S&Ls in this measure in the third year after merger. Despite this change. however, there is no significant difference in the change in the personnel compensation-to-*total deposits* ratio over the three-year, postmerger period. This latter measure is more indicative of the change in operating efficiency of the S&Ls than the portion of operating expenses devoted to personnel compensation.

Analysis of two-year postmerger results

As Table 32 shows, the two-year results (both in differences between the two groups, column 5, and in differences in changes, column 7) are generally consistent with the three-year results. However, one area of difference between the two-year results and three-year results is in the liability structures of the acquiring and nonmerging S&Ls. In the two-year period after merger, acquiring S&Ls financed a significantly higher proportion of their assets through FHLB advances and other borrowing, and less through deposits than the nonmerging S&Ls. By the third year after merger, however, the differences between acquiring and nonmerging S&Ls in total deposits to total assets, advances to total assets, and borrowings to total assets became insignificant. Although this evidence is still somewhat tenuous, it suggests that the acquiring S&Ls use external funds to support themselves while they absorb the acquisition, and subsequently return toward their relative premerger financing pattern.

Multivariate comparisons of acquiring and nonmerging S&Ls

Tables 33 and 34 show results of the two-group discriminant analysis tests for two years after the merger year and three years after the merger year, respectively. The results for the two-year, postmerger model show that the original two-year sample was predicted with 72.3 percent accuracy but that the holdout sample was predicted with 62.5 percent accuracy. The 62.5 percent is, however, significant at the 5.7 percent level ($Z = 1.58$).[7]

Table 33B shows that the discriminant function is significant at less than the 0.001 level. Based on the standardized discriminant function coefficients shown in 33C, the log mean deposit account size, cash plus demand deposits to total assets, government insured mortgages to total mortgages, and personnel compensation to operating expenses are estimated to be the most important discriminators between acquiring and nonmerging S&Ls, in that order.

The results of the three-year discriminant analysis are somewhat different from those of the two-year discriminant analysis. Table 34C shows that the two groups were separated somewhat better in the three-year model than the two-year model in both the original sample and the holdout sample. The predicted classifications in the holdout sample are 67.5 percent correct, which is significant at the 1.4 percent level ($Z = 2.21$). As with the two-year test, the discriminant function of the three-year test is significant at less than the 0.001 level (Table 34B). The variables in the discriminant function are different in the two tests in

Table 33
RESULTS OF THE TWO-GROUP DISCRIMINANT ANALYSIS
TWO YEARS AFTER THE YEAR OF MERGER

A.

Actual Group Membership			Predicted Group Membership			
			Acquiring S&Ls		Nonmerging S&Ls	
Category		Number	Number	%	Number	%
Original: Acquiring S&Ls		63	47	74.6	16	25.4
Nonmerging S&Ls		63	19	30.2	44	69.8
Holdout: Acquiring S&Ls		20	14	70.0	6	30.0
Nonmerging S&Ls		20	9	45.0	11	55.0

Correct classifications, original sample = 72.2%
Correct classifications, holdout group = 62.5%

B.

Eigenvalue	Canonical Correlation	Wilks's Lambda	Chi-Square	DF	Significance
0.32951	0.498	0.7522	33.893	10	0.000+

C.

Variable	Standardized Discriminant Function Coefficients
Log mean deposit account size	−0.22025
Single family mortgages/total mortgages	0.14485
FHA and VA mortgages/total mortgages	−0.17614
Cash plus demand deposits/total assets	−0.17670
Total deposits/total assets	−0.11221
Proportion of depositors above insured limit	0.09905
Net income/total assets	−0.16040
Personnel compensation/operating expenses	0.17316
Operating expenses/operating income	−0.16243
Personnel compensation/total deposits	−0.13515

Table 34
RESULTS OF THE TWO-GROUP DISCRIMINANT ANALYSIS
THREE YEARS AFTER THE YEAR OF MERGER

A.

Actual Group Membership			Predicted Group Membership			
			Acquiring S&Ls		Nonmerging S&Ls	
Category		Number	Number	%	Number	%
Original: Acquiring S&Ls		63	49	77.8	14	22.2
Nonmerging S&Ls		63	17	27.0	46	73.0
Holdout: Acquiring S&Ls		20	14	70.0	6	30.0
Nonmerging S&Ls		20	7	35.0	13	65.0

Correct classifications, original sample = 75.4%
Correct classifications, holdout group = 67.5%

B.

Eigenvalue	Canonical Correlation	Wilks's Lambda	Chi-Square	DF	Significance
0.46431	0.563	0.6829	44.622	14	0.000–

C.

Variable	Standardized Discriminant Function Coefficients
Single family mortgages/total mortgages	0.06383
FHA and VA mortgages/total mortgages	−0.04096
Total mortgages/total assets	−0.18253
Cash plus demand deposits/total assets	−0.07237
Real estate owned and in judgment/total assets	0.05392
FHLB advances/total assets	−0.05396
Interest income on mortgages/total mortgages	−0.10112
Operating income/total assets	0.10631
Net income/total assets	−0.04307
Income on mortgages/gross income	0.18916
Personnel compensation/operating expenses	0.10746
Advertising expenses/operating expenses	0.05585
Personnel compensation/total deposits	−0.02548
Deposit interest on total deposits	−0.12551

several respects, however. Whereas the log mean deposit account size is included in the two-year results, it is not included as a variable in the three-year results. Eight of the fourteen variables in the three-year results are not included in the two-year results, and three of the variables in the two-year results are not included in the three-year results. The three most important discriminant function variables in the three-year results are the ratios of income on mortgages to gross income, of total mortgages to total assets, and of deposit interest to total deposits. None of these variables is in the discriminant function of the two-year results.

These relationships suggest that the characteristic differences between acquiring and nonmerging S&Ls are stronger after the merger than before the merger.[8] In addition, in comparing the S&Ls after the merger, financial measures must be used in different groups and in different ways to distinguish between acquiring and nonmerging S&Ls, depending on how long a period after the merger year is being analyzed.

Comparisons of deposit growth rates

Table 35 shows the average annual deposit growth rates of the acquiring and nonmerging S&Ls from the year end before the merger year to two years and three years after the year of merger.

Two measures are used for the acquiring S&Ls in comparing their growth rates to those of the nonmerging S&Ls. For the A measure, the relevant expression is

$$D_{-1}(1+r)^{j+1} = D_j - \sum_{i=u}^{j} A_i$$

and the expression was solved for r, where j is the number of years after the merger year (either 2 or 3), D is the total deposits of the acquiring firm, and A represents deposit increases brought about through acquisitions. The year of merger is year zero. It should be noted that 13 of the 83 acquiring S&Ls made acquistions after year zero (and thus made more than one acquisition over the period). Measure A assumes no growth for acquired deposits. For measure B, the relevant expression is

$$D_{-1}(1+r)^{j+1} = D_j - \sum_{i=0}^{j} A_i (1+r)^{j-i}$$

and the expression was solved for r. Measure B assumes that acquired deposits grow at the same average annual rate as the original deposits of the acquiring S&Ls over the two-year ($j=2$) or three-year ($j=3$) period after the merger year.

For the nonmerging S&Ls, the following expressions is solved for r:

$$D_{-1}(1+r)^{j+1} = D_j,$$

where j is either 2 or 3.

Table 35 shows that when it is assumed that acquired deposits do not grow, the average annual deposit growth rate of the acquiring S&Ls is 15.1 percent for two years and 14.1 percent for three years after the merger year. This compares to 13.1 percent and 11.7 percent for the nonmerging S&Ls, respectively. The difference in the acquiring associations' growth rate over the nonmerging associations' growth rate is insignificant at less than the 0.01 level.

Table 35
AVERAGE ANNUAL DEPOSIT GROWTH RATES FOR
NONMERGING AND ACQUIRING
SAVINGS AND LOAN ASSOCIATIONS
(In Percentage)

Extent of Period past Merger Year*	Nonmerging S&Ls	Acquiring S&Ls	
		A†	B†
End of 2nd Year	13.1 (8.7)	15.1 (7.7)	13.1 (6.9)
End of 3rd Year	11.7 (8.0)	14.1 (7.1)	12.1 (6.1)

	t Ratio	
	2-1	3-1
2 years	6.34‡	0.03
3 years	6.67‡	0.96

*Period begins with yearend preceding merger year.

†The *A* measure is the average annual growth rate in deposits, excluding increased in deposits through acquisitions. the *B* measure is the average annual growth rate in deposits, excluding deposits through acquisitions and an estimated growth rate of the acquired deposits. The numbers in parentheses represent standard deviations.

‡Significant at the 0.01 level.

When it is assumed that the acquired deposits grow at the same average annual rate as the original deposits of the acquiring S&Ls, however, the average annual growth rate of the acquiring S&Ls decreases to 13.1 percent for two years and 12.1 percent for three years, respectively. It is then found that there is *no* significant difference in the deposit growth rates of the acquiring and nonmerging S&Ls.

On the basis of these results we must conclude that under growth measure *B*, which is probably more theoretically sound, when we control for increases in deposits brought about by acquisitions, acquiring and nonmerging S&Ls experienced rates of deposit growth are approximately equal.

NOTES

1. See Baruch Lev and Gershon Mandelker, "The Microeconomic Consequences of Corporate Mergers," *Journal of Business*, Jan. 1972, pp. 87-88, for a theoretical discussion of the use of the paired group sampling model in analyzing the performance of merging firms.

2. The discriminant analysis package of SPSS was used in this test. See Norman H. Nie, et al., *Statistical Package for the Social Sciences* (New York: McGraw-Hill, 1975), pp. 434-67. The forward stepwise selection process is used in all of the discriminant analysis exercises in this study. A brief description is as follows: The process first chooses the single variable which maximizes the Mahalonobis Distance (D) between the groups. This variable is then paired with each of the other variables, one at a time, and D is computed. The new variable which in conjunction with the initial variable produces the best D-value is selected as the second variable to enter the discriminant function. This procedure of locating the next variable that would yield the best D-value, given the variables already selected, continues until no additional variables provide a minimum level of improvement. As variables are selected for inclusion, some variables previously selected may lose their discriminating power and are dropped from the discriminant function.

3. The same conclusions were reached when two-group discriminant analysis models (acquired-nonmerging, acquiring-acquired, nonmerging-acquired) were run.

4. See D. Morrison, "On the Interpretation of Discriminant Analysis," *Journal of Marketing Research*, May 1969, on this point.

5. Morrison, "On...Discriminant Analysis," discusses the significance of discriminating ability of the discriminant model.

6. This is based on a Z-test as follows:

$$Z = \frac{C - .5}{[.5(1-.5)]\frac{1/2,}{40}}$$

where C is the proportion of correct estimates.

7. Recall that in the year before merger, the financial measures could not be used to distinguish between the two groups to any significant extent.

V

CONCLUSION

Concentration and Merger Policy

We have found that during 1969-74, several characteristics of mergers in the savings and loan industry have changed. First, Federal Home Loan Bank Board policy has enabled federal S&Ls to merge at a rate higher than that of any post-World War II period. Second, the merger rate of state stock S&Ls, although still high over the period of 1969 through 1974, decreased significantly in 1973 and 1974. This decrease occured mainly because of a change in policy of the California savings and loan commissioner regarding mergers of state stock associations. Third, in conjunction with the higher rate of merger of federal S&Ls, the mean asset size of acquiring S&Ls increased substantially over the period. Fourth, the Board's apparent policy of decreasing the number of very small S&Ls led to a substantial decrease in the number of state mutual S&Ls. State mutual S&Ls were those which had a disproportionately higher number of the very small associations.

Implications

First, it is felt that in the future, the areas of major concern in terms of anticompetitive effects of merger will be in those mergers involving federal S&Ls and state stock S&Ls as acquiring institutions. These types of acquisition have involved associations having the largest asset and deposit size. Second, one by-product of allowing federal S&Ls to issue capital stock, which is occurring to a limited extent at present, is a greater rate of merger for the savings and loan industry, especially those mergers involving state stock and federal S&Ls. This relationship will tend to increase the potential concentration in the savings and loan industry. Presently, state stock S&Ls cannot acquire federal mutual or state mutual S&Ls.

89

Third, the policy of decreasing the number of very small associations has increased the number of S&Ls under direct Bank Board regulation as opposed to dual Bank Board and state regulation. To the extent that this effect is desirable, such a policy is advantageous.[1]

Financial Characteristics of Acquiring and Acquired Savings and Loans

Acquiring S&Ls differed significantly from acquired S&Ls in several important respects. First, acquiring S&Ls hold a lower proportion of their investments in single-family mortgages and a higher percentage in insured (FHA and VA) mortgages. Second, the average size of mortgages and the average deposit size of acquiring S&Ls were substantially higher than those for acquired S&Ls. Third, acquiring S&Ls had lower personnel expenses and higher advertising expenses than acquired S&Ls. Finally, the evidence indicates that acquiring S&Ls were more efficient than the acquired S&Ls in terms of operations.

Implications

There are two policy implications in the above findings. First, the mergers that took place in 1969-74 appear to involve less pure horizontal concentration than that described in the theory.[2] That is, the investment characteristics and financial structures of S&Ls differed in several respects. Thus, the mergers resulted in the acquiring S&Ls' increasing competition in *new* markets instead of old markets, which caused less anticompetitive concern than mergers involving S&Ls having the same investment and financing patterns.

Of course determining potential concentration in a consideration of merger applications depends on how "markets" are defined. Presently, the Bank Board considers the total of all home mortgages and the total savings deposits in the relevant geographical area in estimating potential anticompetitive danger of a given merger.[3] Although this consideration has some justification, a more theoretically sound approach would consider the percentage of specific types of mortgage within the relevant geographical area. The above evidence leads us to conclude that S&Ls differ significantly in the type of mortgages for which they compete.

As to the second policy implication in these findings, the greater efficiency of the acquiring S&Ls would lead us to conclude that the recent mergers have been desirable because less efficient S&Ls have been absorbed into more efficient S&Ls. Thus, the assets and liabilities absorbed are to be more soundly managed and controlled, the results of this study would imply.

Performance of Acquiring and Nonmerging S&Ls

Analysis of premerger characteristics indicates that the acquiring S&Ls differed from the matched nonmerging S&Ls in several respects. In terms of asset distribution, acquiring S&Ls invested more in single-family mortgages and less in FHA and VA mortgages than did nonmerging S&Ls. In addition, acquiring S&Ls held a higher proportion of their assets in mortgages and a lower proportion of their assets in cash and demand deposits than did nonmerging S&Ls. The study also found that the ratio of real estate owned and in judgment to total mortgages was lower for the acquiring S&Ls than for the nonmerging S&Ls. In terms of income and cost structure, acquiring S&Ls had a higher ratio of gross operating income to total assets and a higher ratio of personnel compensation to total deposits than did the nonmerging S&Ls.

Despite the differences observed, discriminant analysis exercises showed that the financial measures observed could not be used together to distinguish between the acquiring and nonmerging S&Ls to any significant extent. In addition, the profitability of the acquiring and nonmerging S&Ls did not differ significantly.

With respect to the postmerger analysis, the changes in performance of the acquiring S&Ls from the premerger period to the three-year, postmerger period differed from those of nonmerging S&Ls in several respects. In terms of balance sheet items, acquiring S&Ls decreased the proportion of real estate owned and in judgment to total mortgages to a significantly smaller extent and increased the proportion of FHLB advances to total assets to a significantly greater extent than did the nonmerging S&Ls.

Prices charged and paid for S&L services in the period following the merger also showed different changes for each group. Specifically, over the postmerger period the average interest rate earned on mortgages for the acquiring S&Ls increased to a significantly greater degree than did that of the nonmerging S&Ls. Meanwhile, the differences in the increase in average rate paid on deposits was insignificant. With respect to operating expenses, it is found that the ratio of personnel compensation expenses to operating expenses increased significantly more for the acquiring S&Ls than for the nonmerging S&Ls.

Despite the significantly larger increase in the average yield on mortgages at acquiring S&Ls, there were no significant differences between acquiring and nonmerging S&Ls in the ratios of net income to assets, net income to gross income, and net income to net worth in the third year after merger. Slight increases in advertising expenses and deposit interest expenses of the acquiring S&Ls probably offset the increases in average mortgage interest rate.

Discriminant analysis exercises showed that acquiring and nonmerging S&Ls were more different overall after the merger in question than before. However, the group of financial measures which best distinguishes between the acquiring and nonmerging S&Ls changed somewhat as the period after the merger lengthened. Finally, the study concluded that there were no significant differences in the growth rates of deposits between the acquiring and nonmerging S&Ls from the year end preceding the merger to two years and three years after the merger year. In these comparisons, the acquired deposits were eliminated from consideration.

Implications

First, as a result of the merger policy implemented by the Federal Home Loan Bank Board, S&Ls which made acquisitions during the 1969 to 1972 period differed in several respects from comparable S&Ls in the premerger period. The apparent aggressiveness of the acquiring S&Ls, however, was *not* reflected in their having more or less desirable asset and liability structures and profit performances compared to matched nonmerging S&Ls, on an overall basis in the premerger period.

Second, during the postmerger period, the acquiring S&Ls increased the rate charged on loans relative to the nonmerging S&Ls, but there was no relative increase in the rate acquiring S&Ls paid on deposits. Many theorists hold that relative increases in the differential between asset returns and liability costs result from increases in market concentration. When one S&L acquires another, an increase in market concentration is directly implied. Therefore, there is evidence that greater market concentration due to merger resulted in a relative increase in mortgage rates paid by borrowers. Such a result is undesirable from a public policy viewpoint.

Despite the relative increase in the differential between the mortgage rate and deposit interest rate for the acquiring S&Ls, the study found the merger did *not* enable the acquiring S&Ls to increase their profitability *rates* more than comparable nonmerging S&Ls. This result has important implications for the investigation of motives behind mergers in the S&L industry. It is often held that firms merge because they find it profitable. It is possible that S&Ls merged because of the *anticipation* of higher profits, but the evidence in this study suggests that S&Ls which made acquisitions during the period did not realize higher profits during the two-year and three-year period following the year of merger.

NOTES

1. No study has been conducted comparing the efficiency of dual regulation, as opposed to state or federal regulation, of S&Ls.

2. See Marshall Kaplan, "A Crucial Economic Variable for Anticompetitive Analysis of Mergers," *Federal Home Loan Bank Journal,* Apr. 1971.

3. *Ibid.;* see also Donald Kaplan, "Conversions, Mergers, and Other Structural Reforms in the Savings and Loan Industry" (unpublished speech), 1974.

BIBLIOGRAPHY

Benston, George J. "Cost of Operations and Economies of Scale in Savings and Loan Associations." In *Study of the Savings and Loan Industry,* edited by Irwin Friend. Washington, D.C.: Government Printing Office, 1969.

Brigham, Eugene F., and Pettit, R. Richardson. "Effects of Structure on Performance of the Savings and Loan Industry." In *Study of the Savings and Loan Industry,* edited by Irwin Friend. Washington, D.C.: Government Printing Office, 1969.

Cole, David W. "Measuring Savings and Loan Profitability." *Federal Home Loan Bank Board Journal,* Oct. 1971.

Federal Reserve Bank of Cleveland. "Bank Merger Activity in the Fourth Federal Reserve District, 1960-1967." *Economic Review,* Mar. 1969.

Gillies, James, and Mittlebach, Frank. *Mergers of Savings and Loan Associations in California.* Research Report No. 1, Real Estate Research Program. Los Angeles, Calif.: University of California, 1959.

Harth, Jean G. "Additional Offices and Facilities of Savings Associations." *Legal Bulletin* [U.S. League of Savings Associations], May 1974.

Hester, Donald D. *Stock and Mutual Associations in the Savings and Loan Industry.* Washington, D.C.: Federal Home Loan Bank Board, 1968.

Horvitz, Paul M., and Schull, Bernard, "The Impact of Branch Banking on Bank Performance." *National Banking Review,* Dec. 1964.

93

Kaplan, Donald M. "Conversions, Mergers, and Other Structural Reforms in the Savings and Loan Industry." Unpublished speech presented at the Annual Meeting of the League of Insured Savings and Loan Associations, Sept. 1974.

Kaplan, Marshall. "A Crucial Economic Variable for Anticompetitive Analysis of Mergers." *Federal Home Loan Bank Journal,* Apr. 1971.

Knight, Frank. "Comparative Reserve Requirements at Member and Nonmember Banks." *Monthly Review,* [Federal Reserve Bank of Kansas City,] Apr. 1974.

Lawrence, Robert J. *The Performance of Bank Holding Companies.* Washington, D.C.: The Board of Governors, Federal Reserve System, 1967.

Lev, Baruch, and Mandelker, Gershon. "The Microeconomic Consequences of Corporate Mergers," *Journal of Business,* Jan. 1972.

Morrison, Donald G. "On the Interpretation of Discriminant Analysis." *Journal of Marketing Research,* May 1969.

Mueller, Dennis C. "A Theory of Conglomerate Mergers." *Quarterly Journal of Economics,* Nov. 1969.

Nie, Norman H. *et al. Statistical Package for the Social Sciences.* New York: McGraw-Hill Book Company, 1975.

Rhoades, S.A., and Yeats, A.J. "Growth, Consolidation, and Mergers in Banking." *Journal of Finance,* Dec. 1974.

Siegel, Sidney. *Nonparametric Statistics.* New York: McGraw-Hill, 1956.

Smith, David L. *Characteristics of Merging Banks.* Staff Economic Study No. 49. Washington, D.C.: Board of Governors of the Federal Reserve System, 1969.